The Big Book of Bible Puzzles

Gospel Light

How to make clean copies from this book

YOU MAY MAKE COPIES OF PORTIONS OF THIS BOOK WITH A CLEAN CONSCIENCE IF:

- you (or someone in your organization) are the original purchaser;
- you are using the copies you make for a noncommercial purpose (such as teaching or promoting a ministry) within your church or organization;
- you follow the instructions provided in this book.

HOWEVER, IT IS ILLEGAL FOR YOU TO MAKE COPIES IF:

- you are using the material to promote, advertise or sell a product or service other than for ministry fund-raising;
- you are using the material in or on a product for sale; or
- you or your organization are **not** the original purchaser of this book.

By following these guidelines you help us keep our products affordable. Thank you.
Gospel Light

Editorial Staff

Publisher, William T. Greig

Senior Consulting Publisher, Dr. Elmer L. Towns

Publisher, Research, Planning and Development, Billie Baptiste

Managing Editor, Lynnette Pennings, M.A.

Senior Consulting Editors, Dr. Gary S. Greig, Wesley Haystead, M.S.Ed.

Senior Editor, Theological and Biblical Issues, Bayard Taylor, M.Div.

Editor, Sheryl Haystead

Editorial Team, Amanda Abbas, Mary Gross, Karen McGraw, Jay Bea Summerfield

Writer, Colleen Kennelly

Illustrators, Colleen Kennelly, Roger Mejia

Contents

BIBLE STORY PUZZLES

BIBLE VERSE PUZZLES
Old Testament

New Testament

WHAT A WEEK!

Genesis 1—2:3

The Challenge → When God created the universe, He was busy! Use the letter and number under each line to find a picture of something God made. Write what's in the picture on the line.

Day 1 = _____ _____
         2-D   1-A

Day 2 = _____
         2-A

Day 3 = _____ _____ _____
         3-A   1-B   3-C

Day 4 = _____ _____
         3-B   2-C

Day 5 = _____ _____
         1-D   1-C

Day 6 = _____ _____
         3-D   2-B

Day 7 = REST!

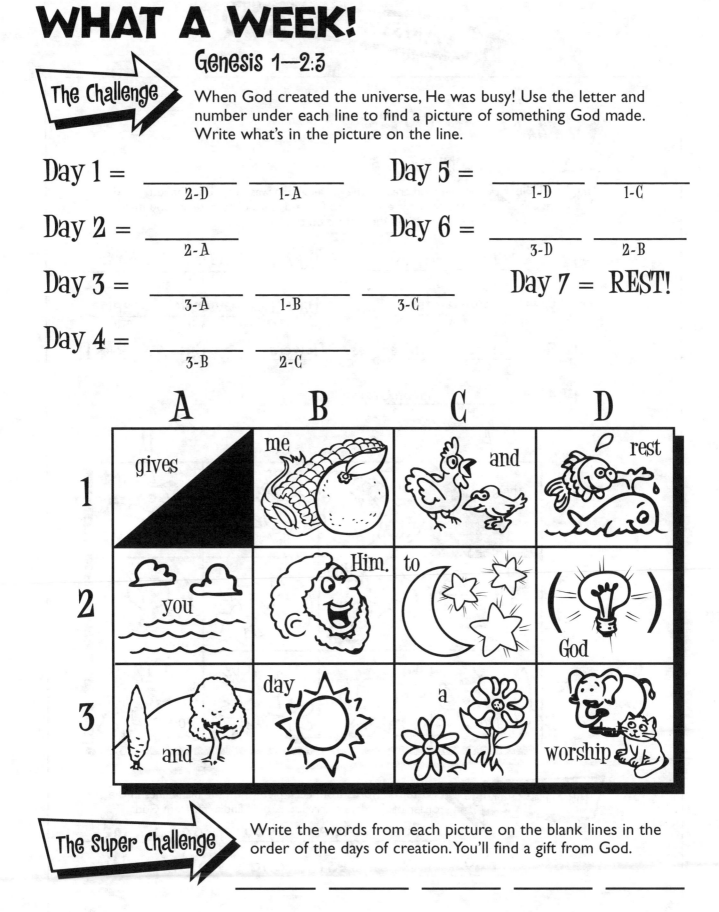

The Super Challenge → Write the words from each picture on the blank lines in the order of the days of creation. You'll find a gift from God.

_____ _____ _____ _____ _____

_____ _____ _____ _____ _____

WHAT A WEEK!

Genesis 1—2:3

The Challenge

When God created the universe, He was busy! Use the letter and number under each line to find a picture of something God made. Write what's in the picture on the line.

Day 1 = <u>light</u> <u>day/night</u>
2-D   1-A

Day 5 = <u>fish</u> <u>birds</u>
1-D   1-C

Day 2 = <u>clouds/water</u>
2-A

Day 6 = <u>animals</u> <u>people</u>
3-D   2-B

Day 3 = <u>trees</u> <u>fruit/veggies</u> <u>flowers</u>
3-A   1-B   3-C

Day 7 = REST!

Day 4 = <u>sun</u> <u>moon/stars</u>
3-B   2-C

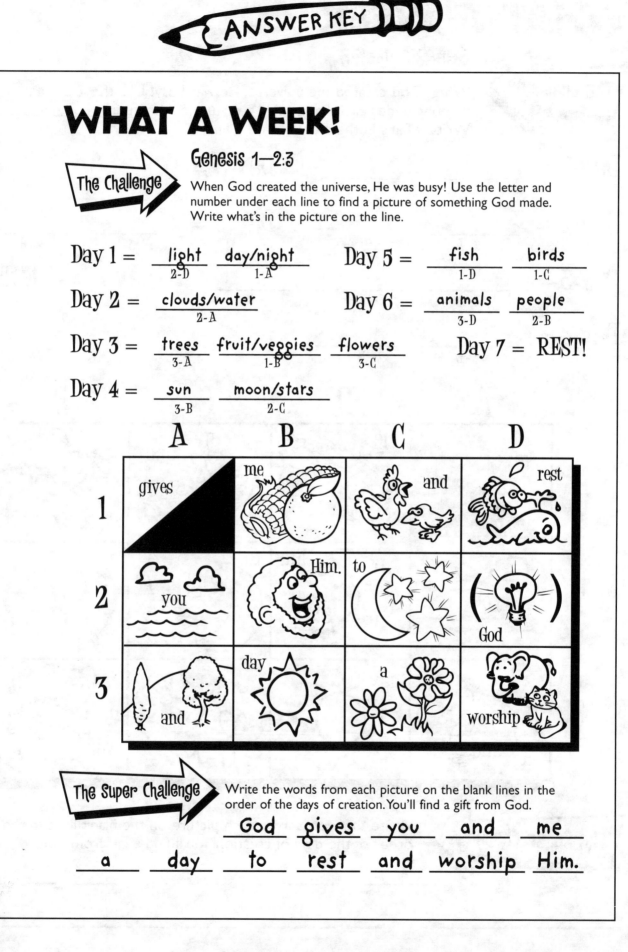

A   B   C   D

The Super Challenge

Write the words from each picture on the blank lines in the order of the days of creation. You'll find a gift from God.

<u>God</u> <u>gives</u> <u>you</u> <u>and</u> <u>me</u>

<u>a</u> <u>day</u> <u>to</u> <u>rest</u> <u>and</u> <u>worship</u> <u>Him.</u>

MADE IN THE SHADE!

Genesis 1:26-31

The Challenge

God created Adam and Eve and gave them the Garden of Eden to live in. Unscramble the words on each insect, and then write the word from each one below the matching insect at the bottom of the page. You'll find out why God created Adam and Eve and you!

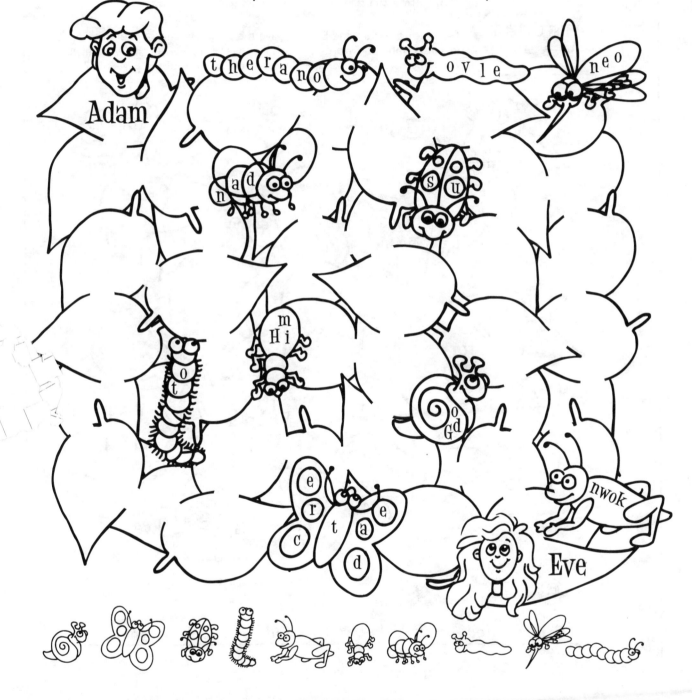

MADE IN THE SHADE!

Genesis 1:26-31

The Challenge → God created Adam and Eve and gave them the Garden of Eden to live in. Unscramble the words on each insect, and then write the word from each one below the matching insect at the bottom of the page. You'll find out why God created Adam and Eve and you!

God created us to know Him and love one another.

OFFERING TIME

The Challenge

Genesis 4:1-16

Double your fun with this maze. Start on the left. You'll discover something important about each of these brothers.

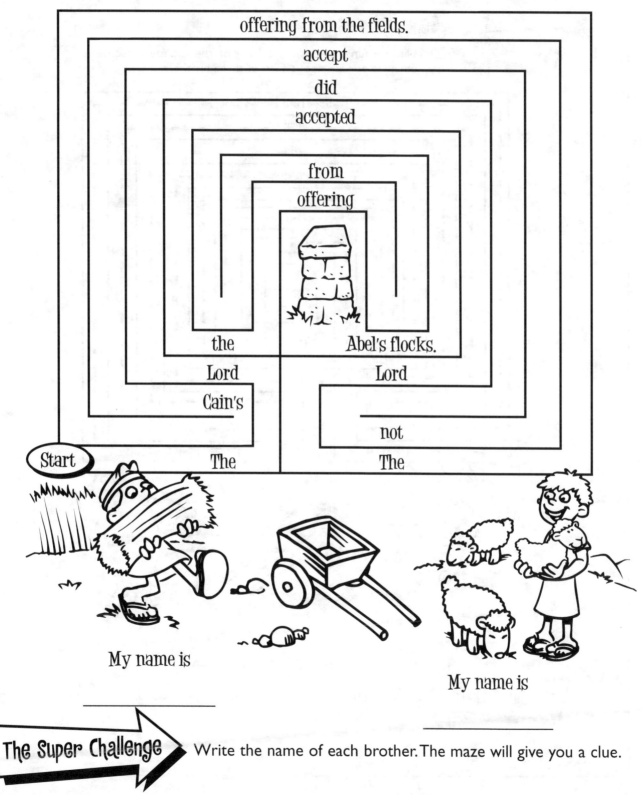

offering from the fields.

accept

did

accepted

from

offering

the   Abel's flocks.

Lord   Lord

Cain's

not

The   The

Start

My name is

My name is

_____   _____

The Super Challenge
Write the name of each brother. The maze will give you a clue.

OFFERING TIME

The Challenge

Genesis 4:1-16

Double your fun with this maze. Start on the left. You'll discover something important about each of these brothers.

offering from the fields.
accept
did
accepted
from
offering
the
Lord
Cain's
Abel's flocks
Lord
not
Start
The
The

My name is
Cain

My name is
Abel

The Super Challenge Write the name of each brother. The maze will give you a clue.

PROMISES, PROMISES!

Genesis 12:1-9;13

The Challenge

Write the first letter of each item in the blank box below it. When you are done, you can read what Abraham learned about God.

The Super Challenge

On the blanks, write the letters from the numbered boxes to find a three-word message.

$$\underline{}_{1} \quad \underline{B}_{2} \quad \underline{Y} \quad \underline{}_{3} \quad \underline{}_{4} \quad \underline{}_{5} \quad \underline{}_{6} \, '$$

$$\underline{}_{7} \quad \underline{}_{1} \quad \underline{}_{8} \quad \underline{}_{5} \, .$$

PROMISES, PROMISES!

Genesis 12:1-9:13

The Challenge

Write the first letter of each item in the blank box below it. When you are done, you can read what Abraham learned about God.

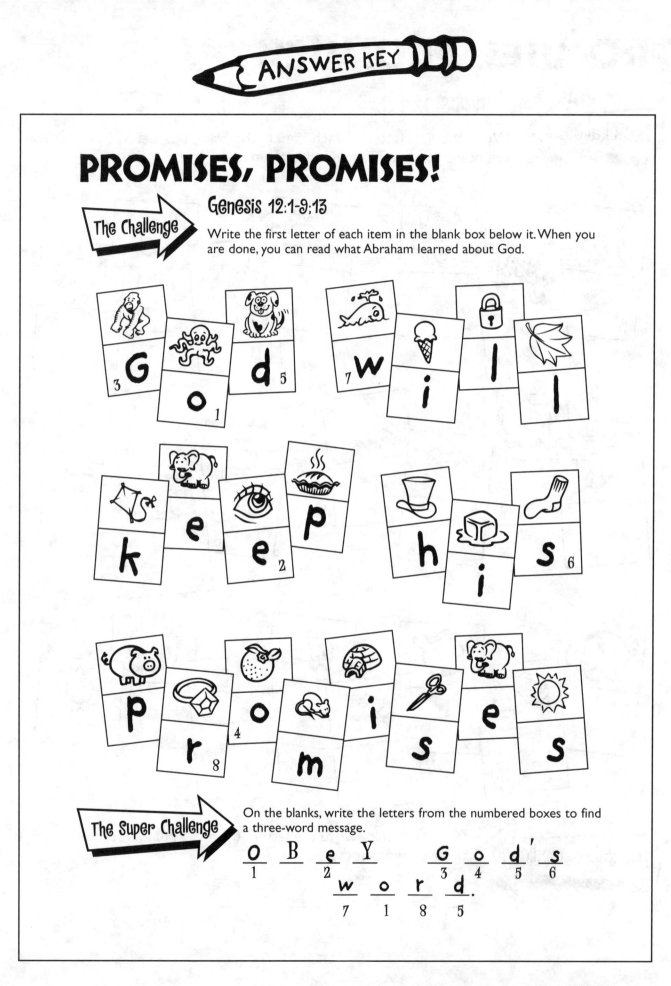

The Super Challenge

On the blanks, write the letters from the numbered boxes to find a three-word message.

O B e Y   G o d ' s
1 2   3 4 5 6

w o r d.
7 1 8 5

OH, BROTHER!

Genesis 37; 41—45

The Challenge

Unscramble the names of Joseph's brothers. (Hint: Read Genesis 35:23-26.) Then choose one brother and draw a line to link him with the brother with the same ID number. Link all the brothers, being careful not to cross any lines when forming your links!

④

Ⓘ E L V
_ _ _ _

①

Ⓞ E H J S E P
_ _ _ _ _ _

②

A D Ⓝ
_ _ _

④

A H S A Ⓒ R I Ⓢ
_ _ _ _ _ _ _

⑤

Ⓐ D G
_ _ _

②

B U L Z U N E
_ _ _ _ _ _

①

H A Ⓢ R E
_ _ _ _ _

③

E Ⓞ S I N M
_ _ _ _ _ _

⑥

H A U J D
_ _ _ _ _

③

E I J Ⓜ N B N A
_ _ _ _ _ _ _

⑥

B E R E N U
_ _ _ _ _ _

⑤

H Ⓟ A I N L T A
_ _ _ _ _ _ _

The Super Challenge

Take the circled letters in the names to spell out the important trait that Joseph showed when dealing with his brothers.

_ _ _ _ _ _ _ _ = _ _ _ _ _ _ _

OH, BROTHER!

Genesis 37; 41—45

The Challenge → Unscramble the names of Joseph's brothers. (Hint: Read Genesis 35:23-26.) Then choose one brother and draw a line to link him with the brother with the same ID number. Link all the brothers, being careful not to cross any lines when forming your links!

1

4

2

O E H J S E P
J O S E P H

A D N
D A N

I E L V
L E V I

4

A H S A C R I S
I S S A C H A R

5

A D G
G A D

2

B U L Z U N E
Z E B U L U N

1

E O S I N M
S I M E O N

3

6

H A U J D
J U D A H

H A S R E
A S H E R

3

E I J M N B N A
B E N J A M I N

6

B E R E N U
R E U B E N

5

H P A I N L T A
N A P T H A L I

The Super Challenge → Take the circled letters in the names to spell out the important trait that Joseph showed when dealing with his brothers.

I O N C A S O S M P = C O M P A S S I O N

I'LL PASS ON THAT!

The Challenge

Exodus 12

Lead Moses to the Hebrew family. Make sure you pass by all the sheep. Avoid the homes of the Egyptians marked by the pharaoh.

The Super Challenge

Write down the words as you pass them, and find what Moses wanted to tell the Hebrew family about God.

_____

I'LL PASS ON THAT!

Exodus 12

The Challenge

Lead Moses to the Hebrew family. Make sure you pass by all the sheep. Avoid the homes of the Egyptians marked by the pharaoh.

The Super Challenge

Write down the words as you pass them, and find what Moses wanted to tell the Hebrew family about God.

Whenever we need help, we can

depend on God's power.

MUSIC TO GOD'S EARS!

Exodus 14—15

Find out what the Israelites sang! Identify each picture below and write what it is in the blanks. Write the circled letter in each numbered word in the matching blank.

1. ☐l☐ e ☐a ⊙f

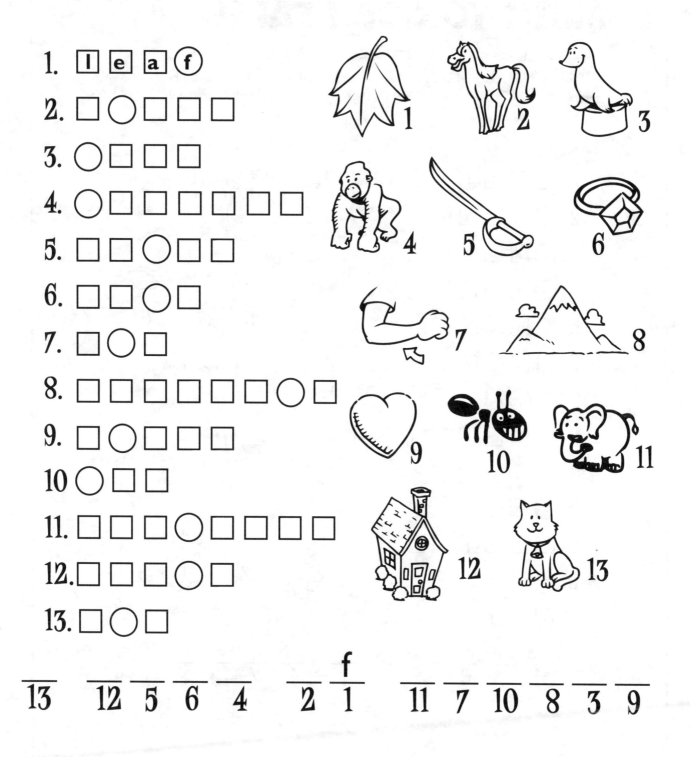

$$\overline{13} \quad \overline{12} \quad \overline{5} \quad \overline{6} \quad \overline{4} \quad \overset{f}{\overline{2}} \quad \overline{1} \quad \overline{11} \quad \overline{7} \quad \overline{10} \quad \overline{8} \quad \overline{3} \quad \overline{9}$$

MUSIC TO GOD'S EARS!

Exodus 14—15

The Challenge ➤ Find out what the Israelites sang! Identify each picture below and write what it is in the blanks. Write the circled letter in each numbered word in the matching blank.

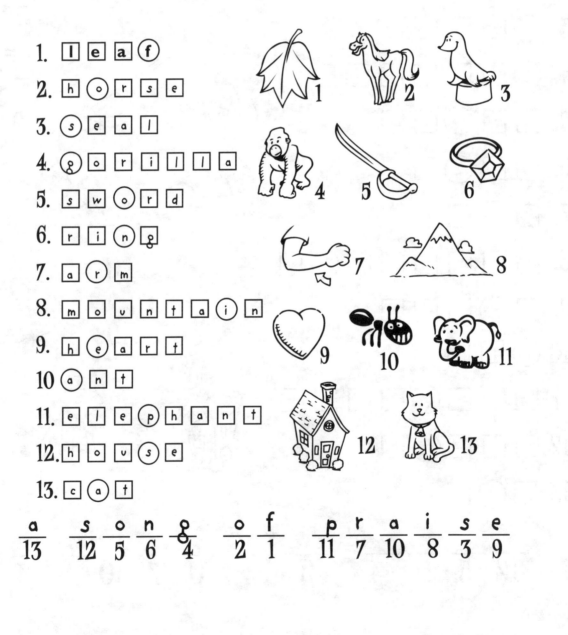

1. l e a **f**
2. h **o** r s e
3. **s** e a l
4. **g** o r i l l a
5. s w **o** r d
6. r i n **g**
7. a **r** m
8. m o u n t a **i** n
9. h **e** a r t
10. **a** n t
11. e l e **p** h a n t
12. h o u s **e**
13. c **a** t

$\dfrac{a}{13}$ $\dfrac{s}{12}$ $\dfrac{o}{5}$ $\dfrac{n}{6}$ $\dfrac{g}{4}$ $\dfrac{o}{2}$ $\dfrac{f}{1}$ $\dfrac{p}{11}$ $\dfrac{r}{7}$ $\dfrac{a}{10}$ $\dfrac{i}{8}$ $\dfrac{s}{3}$ $\dfrac{e}{9}$

MANNA MANIA!

Exodus 16

The Challenge The manna provided by God has been topped with garlic bits. (Phew!) The garlic bits have numbers and letters on them. Write the letters in the blanks below to discover God's message to people all over the world!

___ ___ ___ ___ ___
1   2   3   4   5

___ ___ ___ ___ ___ ___
6   7   8   9   10   11

___ ___ ___ ___ ___ ___ ___ ___ ___ ___ .
12 13 14 15 16 17 18 19 20 21

The Super Challenge Seven children want to share the manna God has given them. None of them cares how big or small their pieces are, but each one wants a piece with three chunks of garlic on it. How can they divide the manna so that everyone is happy? Use only three cuts.

MANNA MANIA!

The Challenge

Exodus 16

The manna provided by God has been topped with garlic bits. (Phew!) The garlic bits have numbers and letters on them. Write the letters in the blanks below to discover God's message to people all over the world!

$$
\begin{array}{cccccc}
T & R & U & S & T \\
\underline{} & \underline{} & \underline{} & \underline{} & \underline{} \\
1 & 2 & 3 & 4 & 5
\end{array}
$$

$$
\begin{array}{ccccc}
G & O & D & F & O & R \\
\underline{} & \underline{} & \underline{} & \underline{} & \underline{} & \underline{} \\
6 & 7 & 8 & 9 & 10 & 11
\end{array}
$$

$$
\begin{array}{cccccccccc}
E & V & E & R & Y & T & H & I & N & G \\
12 & 13 & 14 & 15 & 16 & 17 & 18 & 19 & 20 & 21
\end{array}
$$

The Super Challenge

Seven children want to share the manna God has given them. None of them cares how big or small their pieces are, but each one wants a piece with three chunks of garlic on it. How can they divide the manna so that everyone is happy? Use only three cuts.

TAKE TWO TABLETS . . .

Exodus 20:1-21

The Challenge → Fill in the words from the word list to finish the Ten Commandments.

T
_____ your mom and dad in what you do and say.

S
Don't _____ anyone— if you do you'll pay!

N
Respect God's day of rest— keep that _____ day!

A
Don't lie about anyone— don't _____ and all that jazz!

I
Don't _____ others' stuff; be glad for what you have!

There's only _____ God; He's the one to serve!   **M**

Your bod's just for your mate; that's how to be _____ !   **I**

He's _____ in everything— idols throw you curves!   **O**

Don't use God's name to _____, watch the words you say.   **U**

Don't _____ what isn't yours— just what your money buys!   **N**

WORD LIST:

holy	gossip	take
one	first	swear
envy	murder	
Respect	wise	

The Super Challenge → Oops! You may have realized the Ten Commandments are out of order. Put them in order and write down the corresponding letter to discover where Moses was when God gave him the commandments.

M _ _ _ _ _ _ _ _ _ _

TAKE TWO TABLETS . . .

Exodus 20:1-21

The Challenge → Fill in the words from the word list to finish the Ten Commandments.

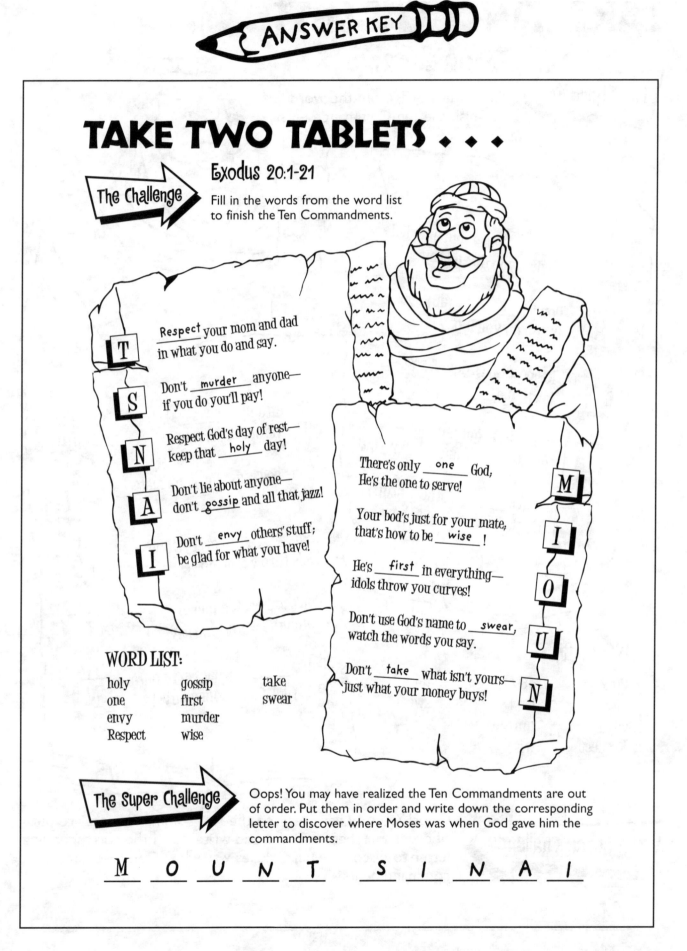

T

<u>Respect</u> your mom and dad in what you do and say.

S

Don't <u>murder</u> anyone— if you do you'll pay!

N

Respect God's day of rest— keep that <u>holy</u> day!

A

Don't lie about anyone— don't <u>gossip</u> and all that jazz!

I

Don't <u>envy</u> others' stuff; be glad for what you have!

There's only <u>one</u> God, He's the one to serve!

M

Your bod's just for your mate, that's how to be <u>wise</u>!

I

He's <u>first</u> in everything— idols throw you curves!

O

Don't use God's name to <u>swear</u>, watch the words you say.

U

Don't <u>take</u> what isn't yours— just what your money buys!

N

WORD LIST:

holy	gossip	take
one	first	swear
envy	murder	
Respect	wise	

The Super Challenge → Oops! You may have realized the Ten Commandments are out of order. Put them in order and write down the corresponding letter to discover where Moses was when God gave him the commandments.

<u>M</u> <u>O</u> <u>U</u> <u>N</u> <u>T</u> <u>S</u> <u>I</u> <u>N</u> <u>A</u> <u>I</u>

SOMETHING IN COMMON!

Ruth

 **The Challenge**

Go around the frame starting at the word "Ruth" and write down every other word. When you've gone around the frame twice, you'll discover something wonderful about Ruth.

Frame words, clockwise from top-left: Ruth · the · cared · way · for · God · Naomi · cares · with · for · her · each · whole · of · heart, · us! · exactly

 **The Super Challenge**

Each of the people above have something in common with the two others in the same row of pictures. All the people in the top row are females. Look at the other rows across, down and diagonally. Can you tell what's alike in each row?

SOMETHING IN COMMON!

The Challenge →

Ruth

Go around the frame starting at the word "Ruth" and write down every other word. When you've gone around the frame twice, you'll discover something wonderful about Ruth.

Ruth | the | cared | way | for
exactly | | | | God
us! | Books | | Hats | Naomi
heart, | | | | cares
of | whole | each | her | for

Words within the picture: Women, Glasses, Men, Pencils, Watches, Striped Shirts

Ruth cared for Naomi with her whole heart, exactly the way God cares for each of us!

The Super Challenge →

Each of the people above have something in common with the two others in the same row of pictures. All the people in the top row are females. Look at the other rows across, down and diagonally. Can you tell what's alike in each row?

PEACE, BROTHER!

1 Samuel 18:1-11

The Challenge

Write in the blanks the first letters of the pictures on the stone wall. Then figure out the missing letters. When you do, you'll find out what God gave David when King Saul wanted to hurt him.

$\overline{}_{5}\ \overline{}_{13}\ \overline{}_{12}\qquad \overline{}_{5}\ \overline{}_{6}\ \overline{}_{10}\ \overline{}_{7}\ \overline{}_{8}\qquad \overline{}_{9}\ \overline{}_{8}$

$\overline{}_{4}\ \overline{}_{13}\ \overline{}_{9}\ \overline{}_{11}\ \overline{}_{1}\ \overline{}_{5}\ \overline{}_{7}\qquad \overline{}_{6}\ \overline{}_{2}$

$\overline{}_{1}\ \overline{}_{14}\ \overline{}_{14}\qquad \overline{}_{8}\ \overline{}_{6}\ \overline{}_{3}\ \overline{}_{9}\ \overline{}_{1}\ \overline{}_{3}\ \overline{}_{6}\ \overline{}_{13}\ \overline{}_{2}\ \overline{}_{8}.$

The Super Challenge
How many triangles can you find hidden in the background? _____

PEACE, BROTHER!

1 Samuel 18:1-11

The Challenge → Write in the blanks the first letters of the pictures on the stone wall. Then figure out the missing letters. When you do, you'll find out what God gave David when King Saul wanted to hurt him.

$$\underset{5}{G}\ \underset{13}{O}\ \underset{12}{D}\qquad \underset{5}{G}\ \underset{6}{I}\ \underset{10}{V}\ \underset{7}{E}\ \underset{8}{S}\qquad \underset{9}{U}\ \underset{8}{S}$$

$$\underset{4}{C}\ \underset{13}{O}\ \underset{9}{U}\ \underset{11}{R}\ \underset{1}{A}\ \underset{5}{G}\ \underset{7}{E}\qquad \underset{6}{I}\ \underset{2}{N}$$

$$\underset{1}{A}\ \underset{14}{L}\ \underset{14}{L}\qquad \underset{8}{S}\ \underset{6}{I}\ \underset{3}{T}\ \underset{9}{U}\ \underset{1}{A}\ \underset{3}{T}\ \underset{6}{I}\ \underset{13}{O}\ \underset{2}{N}\ \underset{8}{S}.$$

The Super Challenge → How many triangles can you find hidden in the background? **52**

I'M OUTTA HERE!

The Challenge

1 Samuel 24

King Saul was so jealous of David, he wanted to get rid of him. David had to run away, but God protected him. Trace the path David took for his escape.

The Super Challenge
Order the words in the clouds to make a sentence about one of God's gifts to us.

I'M OUTTA HERE!

1 Samuel 24

The Challenge King Saul was so jealous of David, he wanted to get rid of him. David had to run away, but God protected him. Trace the path David took for his escape.

The Super Challenge Order the words in the clouds to make a sentence about one of God's gifts to us.

God gives us courage to love our enemies.

FINDERS KEEPERS

The Challenge →

2 Samuel 6

Order the seven words found in the puzzle below to write a sentence about what believers do when they get together.

_____ _____ _____ _____ _____ _____ _____.

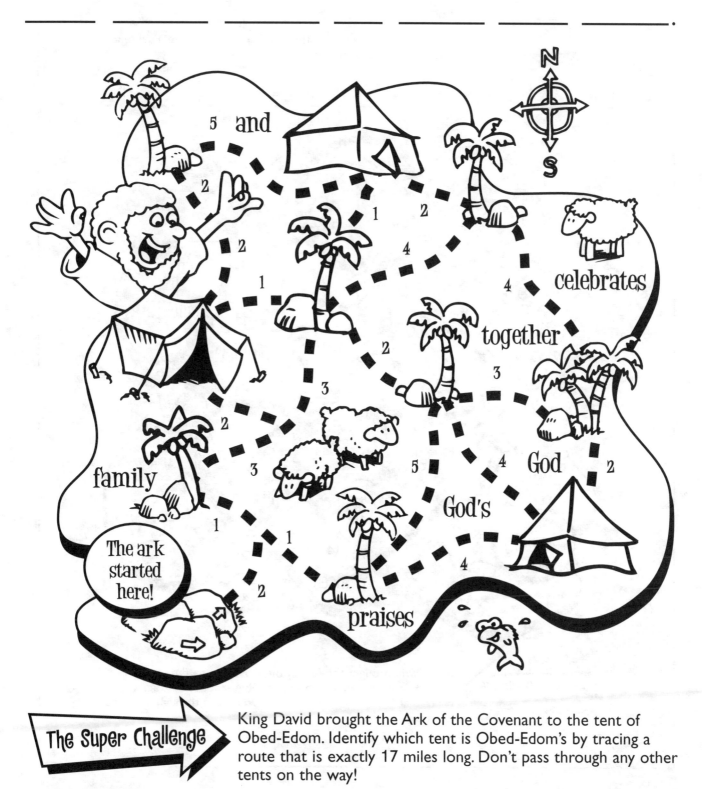

The Super Challenge →

King David brought the Ark of the Covenant to the tent of Obed-Edom. Identify which tent is Obed-Edom's by tracing a route that is exactly 17 miles long. Don't pass through any other tents on the way!

FINDERS KEEPERS

The Challenge

2 Samuel 6

Order the seven words found in the puzzle below to write a sentence about what believers do when they get together.

God's   family   celebrates   and   praises   God   together .

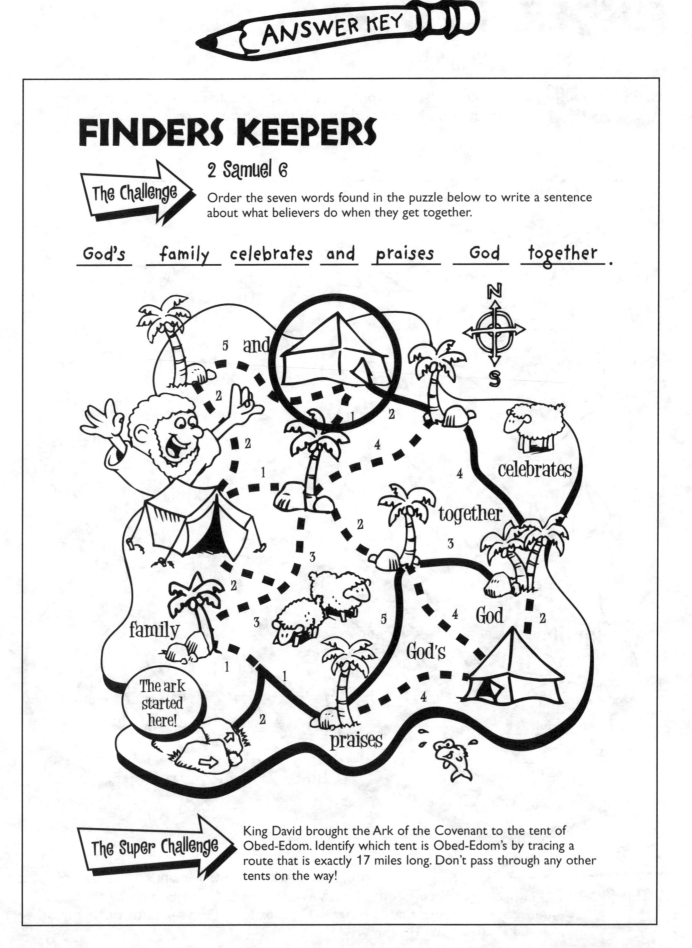

The Super Challenge

King David brought the Ark of the Covenant to the tent of Obed-Edom. Identify which tent is Obed-Edom's by tracing a route that is exactly 17 miles long. Don't pass through any other tents on the way!

SOLOMON, THE WISE GUY!

The Challenge

1 Kings 3:1-15

Starting with the white G, follow the building blocks around the Temple, writing down every other letter. When you've worked your way around, go back by starting at the G on the bottom. When you've been around the Temple twice, you will have written Solomon's prayer.

Solomon's Prayer:

___ ____ ____ ____ ____

_____ , __ __ __ ___

___ ____ _____ ____ ___ __ ___ .

The Super Challenge ➤ On the Temple floor, find these words describing wise ways to live:

faith   gratitude   humility   joy   love
patience   peace   trust   truth   wisdom

SOLOMON, THE WISE GUY!

1 Kings 3:1-15

 **The Challenge** Starting with the white G, follow the building blocks around the Temple, writing down every other letter. When you've worked your way around, go back by starting at the G on the bottom. When you've been around the Temple twice, you will have written Solomon's prayer.

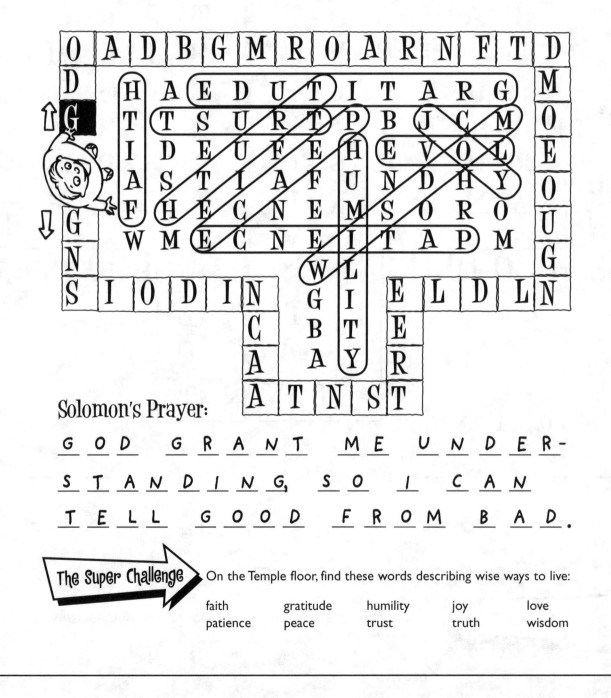

Solomon's Prayer:

G O D G R A N T M E U N D E R-

S T A N D I N G, S O I C A N

T E L L G O O D F R O M B A D.

The Super Challenge On the Temple floor, find these words describing wise ways to live:

faith	gratitude	humility	joy	love
patience	peace	trust	truth	wisdom

PICK-UP STICKS!

1 Kings 5—8

The builders of the Temple used a lot of logs to build the Temple. To solve this puzzle, pretend you're playing Pick-up Sticks. "Pick" up the log that's on top of the pile. Write the word on it in the first blank below. If you pick up the logs in the correct order, you'll spell out why we can worship God. (The first one is done for you.)

God _____ _____

_____ _____

_____ _____

_____ _____

_____ _____

_____ _____

The Super Challenge   How many squares can you find on the Temple? _____

PICK-UP STICKS!

1 Kings 5—8

The Challenge → The builders of the Temple used a lot of logs to build the Temple. To solve this puzzle, pretend you're playing Pick-up Sticks. "Pick" up the log that's on top of the pile. Write the word on it in the first blank below. If you pick up the logs in the correct order, you'll spell out why we can worship God.

These each have two!

God   will

always   be

a   protector

in   your   time

of   trouble   or

of   need.

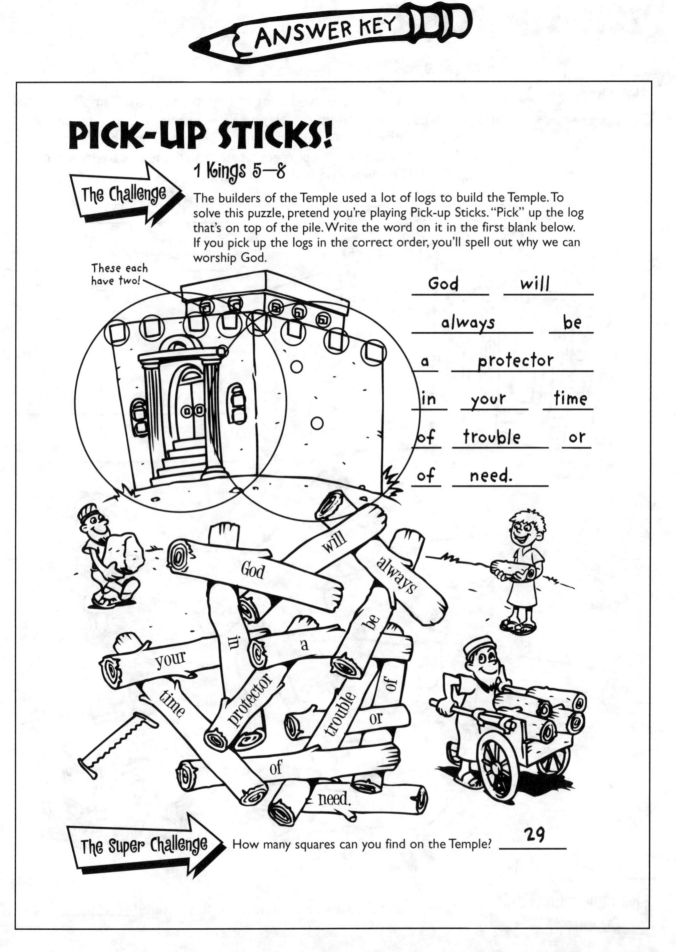

The Super Challenge → How many squares can you find on the Temple? _____ 29

JAM SESSION!

2 Chronicles 20:1-30

The Challenge → Follow the path from each musician and write the letters below each instrument and on the blank lines. Read the phrase to find out why Jehoshaphat asked the musicians to play music.

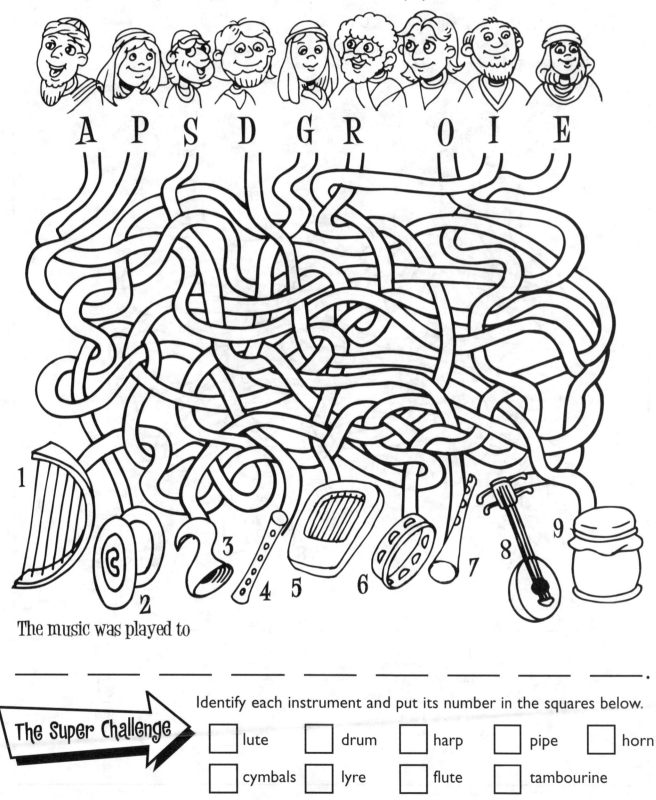

A P S D G R O I E

The music was played to

_____ _____ _____ _____ _____ _____ _____ _____ _____ .

The Super Challenge → Identify each instrument and put its number in the squares below.

☐ lute ☐ drum ☐ harp ☐ pipe ☐ horn

☐ cymbals ☐ lyre ☐ flute ☐ tambourine

JAM SESSION!

2 Chronicles 20:1-30

The Challenge → Follow the path from each musician and write the letters below each instrument and on the blank lines. Read the phrase to find out why Jehoshaphat asked the musicians to play music.

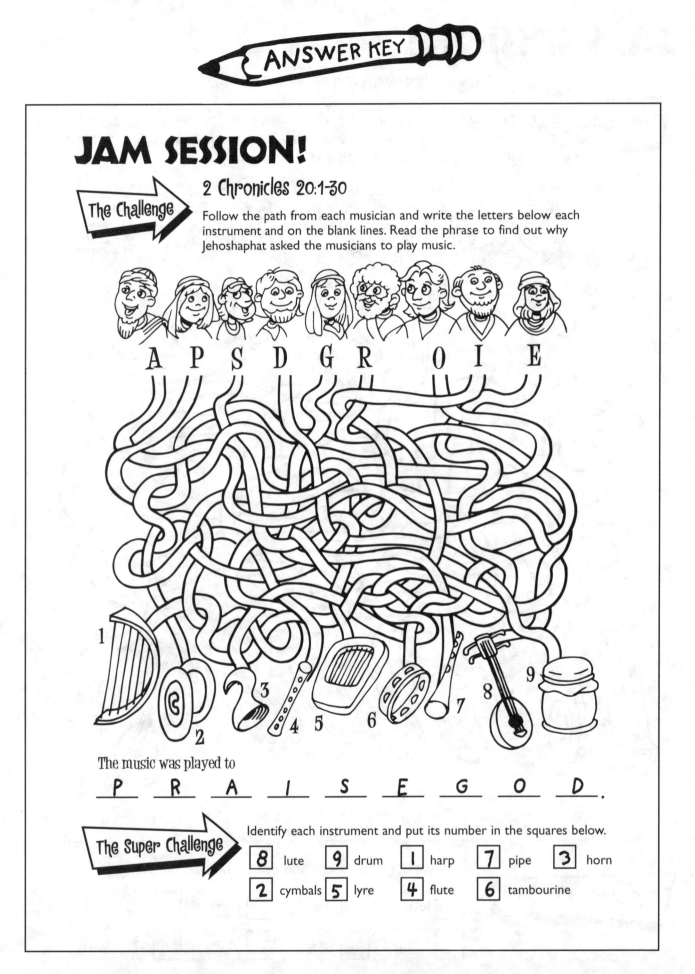

A P S D G R O I E

The music was played to

P R A I S E G O D.

The Super Challenge → Identify each instrument and put its number in the squares below.

| 8 | lute | 9 | drum | 1 | harp | 7 | pipe | 3 | horn |
| 2 | cymbals | 5 | lyre | 4 | flute | 6 | tambourine |

STORY TIME!

The Challenge

2 Chronicles 34—35

The kids have written the story of their time at the Passover feast, but they mixed up some of the words. Figure it out to read the story.

I ⬜remember⬜ when we went to the verPasso feast near the pleTem. ⬜What⬜ a day! The estpri
_____ _____

was excited about the goodness of ⬜God.⬜ He wore long elegant esrob of plepur and ldgo.
_____ _____ ____

After ingpray at the taral, he ⬜has⬜tily came out and proclaimed the tionbracele. When he was
_____ _____ _____

⬜done,⬜ everyone chedeer and started to isepra God. At the feast, I ate lots of tableveges.
_____ _____ _____

After eating, we ceddan be⬜for⬜e the Lord. Later we ate the Passover mbla. My father was one
_____ _____

of the erssing. It was a eatgr day. It was the rstfi time the Passover had been celebrated since
_____ _____ _____

Samuel the phetpro was alive. ⬜You⬜ should have seen it! I still had vense days of fun ⬜and⬜ the
_____ _____

astFe of Unleavened eadBr to enjoy. ⬜Praise⬜ God. I love ⬜Him⬜ !
_____ _____

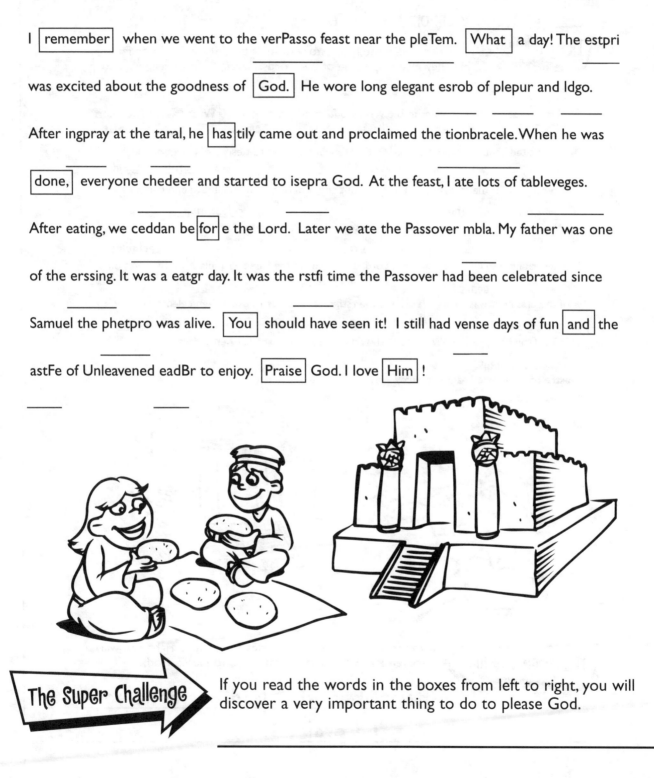

The Super Challenge

If you read the words in the boxes from left to right, you will discover a very important thing to do to please God.

_____

_____

STORY TIME!

2 Chronicles 34—35

The Challenge

The kids have written the story of their time at the Passover feast, but they mixed up some of the words. Figure it out to read the story.

I [remember] when we went to the verPasso feast near the pleTem. [What] a day! The estpri
_____Passover_____Temple_____priest

was excited about the goodness of [God.] He wore long elegant esrob of plepur and ldgo.
_____robes__purple__gold

After ingpray at the taral, he [has] tily came out and proclaimed the tionbracele. When he was
_____praying___altar_____celebration

[done,] everyone chedeer and started to isepra God. At the feast, I ate lots of tableveges.
_____cheered_____praise_____vegetables

After eating, we ceddan be[for]e the Lord. Later we ate the Passover mbla. My father was one
_____danced_____lamb

of the erssing. It was a eatgr day. It was the rstfi time the Passover had been celebrated since
_____singers_____great_____first

Samuel the phetpro was alive. [You] should have seen it! I still had vense days of fun [and] the
_____prophet_____seven

astFe of Unleavened eadBr to enjoy. [Praise] God. I love [Him]!

Feast_____Bread

The Super Challenge

If you read the words in the boxes from left to right, you will discover a very important thing to do to please God.

Remember what God has done for you and praise Him.

BUILDING BLOCKS

Nehemiah 3

The Challenge >

God wants us to help each other. Follow the directions in the arrows to help the water bearer get through the maze so that she can give the thirsty worker a drink.

The Super Challenge >

Unscramble the words in the rocks for some important words from God.

_____

_____.

BUILDING BLOCKS

Nehemiah 3

The Challenge → God wants us to help each other. Follow the directions in the arrows to help the water bearer get through the maze so that she can give the thirsty worker a drink.

Start

Finish

herotan

od

oen

odGs

aysalw

ot

rkwo

ragecouen

The Super Challenge → Unscramble the words in the rocks for some important words from God.

Always encourage one another to do God's work

FEAST ON THIS!

The Challenge ➤

Nehemiah 8

God commanded the children of Israel to take some special time off to celebrate! Cool, huh? Unscramble the letters on the flags to find out what the Israelites said about God's command to feast and rest.

K T A H N   U Y O   D G O

___ ___ ___ ___ ___ ___ ___ ___ ___ , ___ ___ ___

The Super Challenge ➤ All the town is ready to celebrate the Feast of Tabernacles. See if you can figure out who owns which booth in the marketplace and what he's providing for the feast. Write each food name in the top of the booth and each man's name in his booth's oval.

Clue 1: Micah has the round-topped booth, to the right of the meat man.

Clue 2: David and Joel's booths are next to each other.

Clue 3: David's booth is right next to Micah's. David sells drinks.

Clue 4: The veggie man's booth is not next to Micah's.

Clue 5: The bread man's booth has a round top.

Clue 6: Simeon's booth is the biggest.

FEAST ON THIS!

The Challenge →

Nehemiah 8

God commanded the children of Israel to take some special time off to celebrate! Cool, huh? Unscramble the letters on the flags to find out what the Israelites said about God's command to feast and rest.

KTAHN UYO DGO

T H A N K   Y O U,   G O D

MEAT — SIMEON

BREAD — MICAH

DRINKS — DAVID

VEGGIES — JOEL

The Super Challenge →

All the town is ready to celebrate the Feast of Tabernacles. See if you can figure out who owns which booth in the marketplace and what he's providing for the feast. Write each food name in the top of the booth and each man's name in his booth's oval.

Clue 1:   Micah has the round-topped booth, to the right of the meat man.

Clue 2:   David and Joel's booths are next to each other.

Clue 3:   David's booth is right next to Micah's. David sells drinks.

Clue 4:   The veggie man's booth is not next to Micah's.

Clue 5:   The bread man's booth has a round top.

Clue 6:   Simeon's booth is the biggest.

PARTY TIME!

Esther

The Challenge ➤ Unscramble the letters to find out why it was important for Esther to be queen.

thsEre caebme enque
_____

os hes oucld
_____

creseu ehr oleppe
_____

omrf tdeha!
_____

The Super Challenge ➤

After the people were saved, there was a big party. Some people at the party described Queen Esther's table. Can you pick out the queen's table from the descriptions?

Timothy saw a big cake with dark icing and six dates on it, and a plate of flatbreads on the table.

James said the flatbreads were triangular. There was a white round dessert dome. But his favorite was the three cupcakes.

Ruth said that Esther's table had four special-shaped cakes and a cloth with spots and stripes.

The queen sat at table _____.

1

2

3

4

PARTY TIME!

Esther

The Challenge →

Unscramble the letters to find out why it was important for Esther to be queen.

thsEre caebme enque
Esther became queen

os hes oucld
so she could

creseu ehr oleppe
rescue her people

omrf tdeha!
from death!

The Super Challenge →

After the people were saved, there was a big party. Some people at the party described Queen Esther's table. Can you pick out the queen's table from the descriptions?

Timothy saw a big cake with dark icing and six dates on it, and a plate of flatbreads on the table. *Can't be table 4. No dark icing.*

James said the flatbreads were triangular. There was a white round dessert dome. But his favorite was the three cupcakes. *Can't be table 2. Flatbreads are square.*

Ruth said that Esther's table had four special-shaped cakes and a cloth with spots and stripes. *Can't be table 1. No spots.*

The queen sat at table **3**.

PROPHET-SHARING

Isaiah 9:1-7; Micah 5:2-5

The Challenge → God chose men called prophets to tell people about Jesus before He was even born! Can you trace this prophet's journey to Bethlehem to see Jesus?

Ready or not, here He comes!

The Super Challenge → Use the map to write down a special message from God for you. The first clue is done for you. Follow the clues to finish your message.

4-F   5-A   2-B   1-D   2-E   3-A   4-D   3-E   3-C   5-F

Cele _____ ___ ___ _____ ___ _____ _____.

PROPHET-SHARING
Isaiah 9:1-7; Micah 5:2-5

Ready or not, here He comes!

The Challenge → God chose men called prophets to tell people about Jesus before He was even born! Can you trace this prophet's journey to Bethlehem to see Jesus?

A   B   C   D   E   F

Start

JERUSALEM ROME

birth

the   of

the   Sav   ised

prom   Cele

brate   ior.   Finish

The Super Challenge → Use the map to write down a special message from God for you. The first clue is done for you. Follow the clues to finish your message.

4-F	5-A	2-B	1-D	2-E	3-A	4-D	3-E	3-C	5-F
Cele brate	the	birth	of	the	prom	ised	Sav	ior.

HUNGRY FOR GOD!

Daniel 1

The Challenge

When Daniel first came to Babylon, he ate only fruit and vegetables. Unscramble the words in the foods and write them in the matching blanks. When you are done, you'll read about Daniel's life.

corn   watermelon

_____

peas   mushrooms   pineapple

cherries   orange   asparagus

grapes .

The Super Challenge

Look at the picture for 30 seconds. Then turn over your paper and write down all the fruits and vegetables you can remember.

HUNGRY FOR GOD!

Daniel 1

The Challenge

When Daniel first came to Babylon, he ate only fruit and vegetables. Unscramble the words in the foods and write them in the matching blanks. When you are done, you'll read about Daniel's life.

Daniel	always	
corn	watermelon	
loved	and	obeyed
peas	mushrooms	pineapple
God	in	all
cherries	orange	asparagus
	things	
	grapes	

The Super Challenge

Look at the picture for 30 seconds. Then turn over your paper and write down all the fruits and vegetables you can remember.

SHAPE YOUR FAITH!

The Challenge

Daniel 2

Find the letter in each shape to discover something all God's children should do.

___ ___ ___ ___ ___ ___ ___   ___ ___ ___ ___

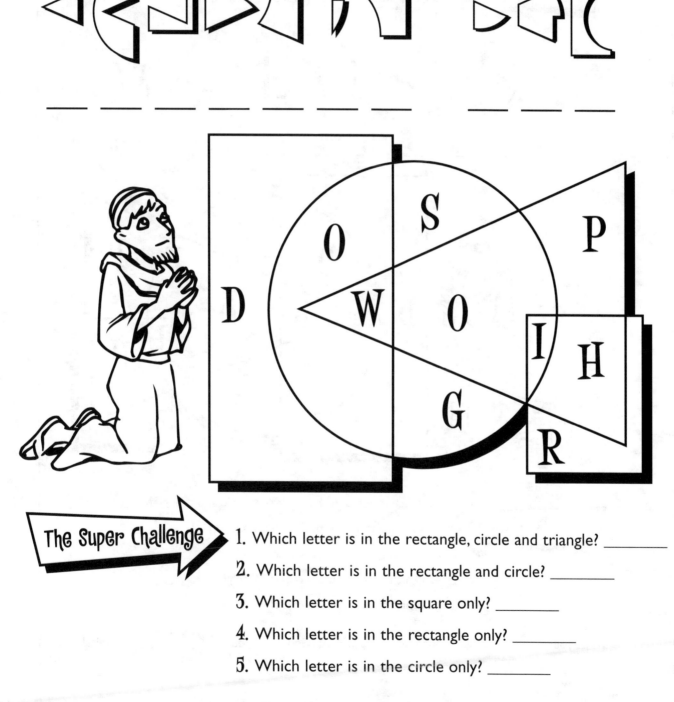

The Super Challenge

1. Which letter is in the rectangle, circle and triangle? _____

2. Which letter is in the rectangle and circle? _____

3. Which letter is in the square only? _____

4. Which letter is in the rectangle only? _____

5. Which letter is in the circle only? _____

Write your answers in order to find one way to worship God: With your _____ of praise!

SHAPE YOUR FAITH!

The Challenge

Daniel 2

Find the letter in each shape to discover something all God's children should do.

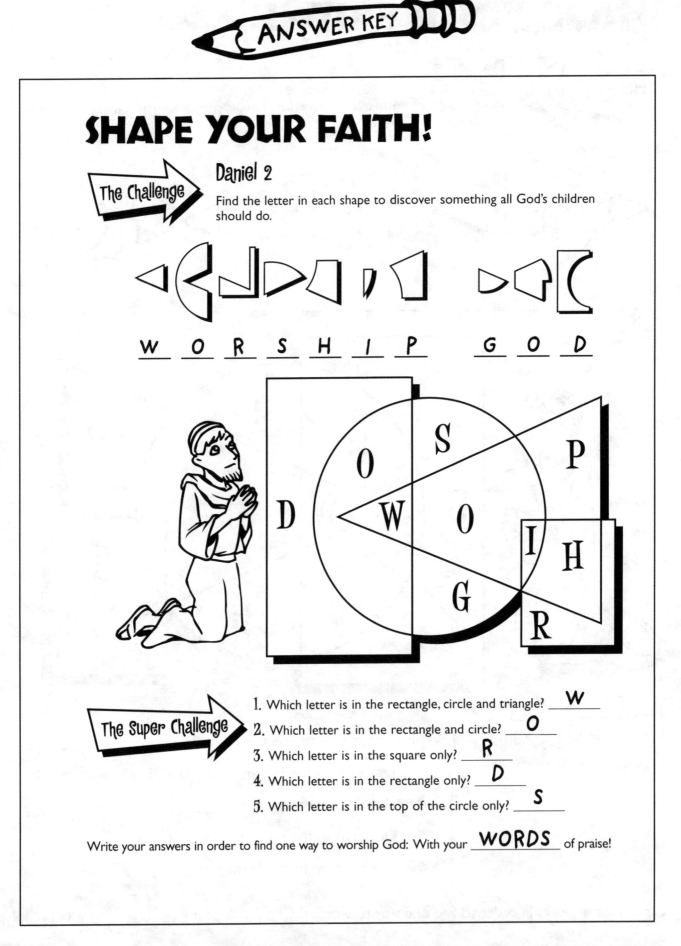

W O R S H I P   G O D

The Super Challenge

1. Which letter is in the rectangle, circle and triangle? __W__
2. Which letter is in the rectangle and circle? __O__
3. Which letter is in the square only? __R__
4. Which letter is in the rectangle only? __D__
5. Which letter is in the top of the circle only? __S__

Write your answers in order to find one way to worship God: With your __WORDS__ of praise!

JONAH'S ALL WASHED UP!

The Challenge

Jonah

Break the code to discover what Jonah said in Jonah 1:9 about God.

The Super Challenge

You know what happened to Jonah. There's something fishy about all the stuff washed up on the beach. Eyeball the picture for a minute; then turn over the page to see how many items from the picture you can write down.

JONAH'S ALL WASHED UP!

The Challenge

Jonah

Break the code to discover what Jonah said in Jonah 1:9 about God.

The Super Challenge

You know what happened to Jonah. There's something fishy about all the stuff washed up on the beach. Eyeball the picture for a minute; then turn over the page to see how many items from the picture you can write down.

THREE MORE WISE GUYS!

Matthew 2:1-12

The shepherd boy has a message about why the wise men came, but he left out all the vowels and the words are all mixed up! Can you add the vowels and put the message in order, so you can understand it?

_____ _____ _____ _____ ____ _____

_____, _____ _____ _____ _____.

The shepherd boy needs to get the camels back to the three wise men, but there's a problem. The boy can only take one camel at a time, because the camels may fight. The smallest camel, Goldie, doesn't like Frank, the biggest camel. Frank doesn't like Myrrh, but Myrrh likes everyone. In what order should the boy take the camels back to the wise men so that there's no fighting between Goldie and Frank?

First I'll bring _____.   **Then I'll bring** _____.

Last I'll bring _____.

THREE MORE WISE GUYS!

Matthew 2:1-12

The Challenge → The shepherd boy has a message about why the wise men came, but he left out all the vowels and the words are all mixed up! Can you add the vowels and put the message in order, so you can understand it?

The ___ wise ___ men ___ came ___ to ___ worship ___

Jesus ___ , the ___ Savior ___ of ___ the ___ world ___ .

Frank

BETHLEHEM

wise came men The

the Jesus to worship

Myrrh

world Savior of the

The Super Challenge → The shepherd boy needs to get the camels back to the three wise men, but there's a problem. The boy can only take one camel at a time, because the camels may fight. The smallest camel, Goldie, doesn't like Frank, the biggest camel. Frank doesn't like Myrrh, but Myrrh likes everyone. In what order should the boy take the camels back to the wise men so that there's no fighting between Goldie and Frank?

First I'll bring __Goldie__ . Then I'll bring __Myrrh__ .
Last I'll bring __Frank__ .

TAKE THE PLUNGE!

Matthew 3:13-17

The Challenge → Help Jesus get to John the Baptist, so He can be baptized in the Jordan River.

Start

is · my · This · I

love;

him

love;

my

whom

with

Son,

I · well

I

am

Son,

"This

I

is

am · well

my · pleased."

pleased.

Finish

The Super Challenge → Write the words you passed as you went through the maze to read what God said about Jesus in Matthew 3:17.

_____

_____

TAKE THE PLUNGE!

Matthew 3:13-17

The Challenge Help Jesus get to John the Baptist, so He can be baptized in the Jordan River.

The Super Challenge Write the words you passed as you went through the maze to read what God said about Jesus in Matthew 3:17.

"This is my Son, whom I love; with him I am well pleased."

GO (TRANS)FIGURE!!

Matthew 17:1-13

The Challenge

When Peter, James and John followed Jesus up a mountain, a strange thing happened: Moses and Elijah appeared with Jesus. Use the words on each sheep to make a sentence about Jesus. (Some of the words are filled in to get you started.)

_____ _____ _____ us _____ _____

to know _____ _____ is

_____ _____

The Super Challenge

Draw three lines, one from Peter to Elijah, one from James to Jesus and one from John to Moses. Easy? Maybe! No lines can cross each other.

GO (TRANS)FIGURE!!

Matthew 17:1-13

 The Challenge

When Peter, James and John followed Jesus up a mountain, a strange thing happened: Moses and Elijah appeared with Jesus. Use the words on each sheep to make a sentence about Jesus. (Some of the words are filled in to get you started.)

Prayer   helps   us   get
to   know   that   Jesus   is
God's   Son.

The Super Challenge Draw three lines, one from Peter to Elijah, one from James to Jesus and one from John to Moses. Easy? Maybe! No lines can cross each other.

THE UNFORGIVING SERVANT

Matthew 18:21-35

When Peter asked Jesus how many times he should forgive someone, Jesus answered "seventy-seven times" (Matthew 18:22).* What did Jesus mean? Find out by writing on each blank line the letter that comes between the two letters below each line.

___ ___ ___ ___ ___ ___ ___
EG NP QS FH HJ UW DF

___ ___ ___ ___ ___ ___   ___ ___ ___ ___
NP SU GI DF QS RT   LN NP QS DF

___ ___ ___ ___ ___   ___ ___ ___ ___
SU HJ LN DF RT   SU GI ZB MO

___ ___ ___   ___ ___ ___
XZ NP TV   BD ZB MO

___ ___ ___ ___ ___!
BD NP TV MO SU

*Some Bible translations say "seventy times seven." How many times would that be? _____
In order to forgive someone that many times in a year, how many times a week would you need to forgive? _____

THE UNFORGIVING SERVANT

Matthew 18:21-35

The Challenge → When Peter asked Jesus how many times he should forgive someone, Jesus answered "seventy-seven times" (Matthew 18:22).* What did Jesus mean? Find out by writing on each blank line the letter that comes between the two letters below each line.

F O R G I V E
EG NP QS FH HJ UW DF

O T H E R S   M O R E
NP SU GI DF QS RT   LN NP QS DF

T I M E S   T H A N
SU HJ LN DF RT   SU GI ZB MO

Y O U   C A N
XZ NP TV   BD ZB MO

C O U N T!
BD NP TV MO SU

The Super Challenge → *Some Bible translations say "seventy times seven." How many times would that be? __490__

In order to forgive someone that many times in a year, how many times a week would you need to forgive? _almost 10 times!_

KIDDING AROUND!

Matthew 19:13-15

The Challenge

Jesus loved everyone, especially children. He showed it through his words and actions. Can you tell what Jesus is saying to these kids by matching the letters to the blanks below?

___ ___ ___   ___ ___ ___
1   2   3   4   5   6

___ ___ ___ ___ ___ ___ ___ ___ ___
7   8   9   10 11 12 13 14 15

___ ___   ___ ___ ___ .
16 17   18 19 20

The Super Challenge Circle 11 things wrong with this picture.

KIDDING AROUND!

Matthew 19:13-15

The Challenge

Jesus loved everyone, especially children. He showed it through his words and actions. Can you tell what Jesus is saying to these kids by matching the letters to the blanks below?

Y O U   A R E
1 2 3   4 5 6

I M P O R T A N T
7 8 9 10 11 12 13 14 15

T O   G O D.
16 17   18 19 20

The Super Challenge Circle 11 things wrong with this picture.

TALENT SCOUT!

The Challenge

Matthew 25:14-30

Jesus told a story about a rich man who gave some talents (money, in this story) to three servants. Follow the path from servant #1 to his money. Write the words you pass (in order) as you go. Do the same for servant #2 and #3. You'll discover what God wants us to learn from this story.

_____

_____

_____

The Super Challenge

The rich man has 22 coins to spend. He can only buy one of the same item. What will he buy?

Bread
4 coins

Turban
14 coins

Meat
7 coins

Water
6 coins

Robe
14 coins

Oil Lamp
5 coins

_____

TALENT SCOUT!

Matthew 25:14-30

The Challenge → Jesus told a story about a rich man who gave some talents (money, in this story) to three servants. Follow the path from servant #1 to his money. Write the words you pass (in order) as you go. Do the same for servant #2 and #3. You'll discover what God wants us to learn from this story.

Use the talents
God gave you to serve Him and others.

The Super Challenge → The rich man has 22 coins to spend. He can only buy one of the same item. What will he buy?

Turban 14 coins
Meat 7 coins
Bread 4 coins
Water 6 coins
Robe 14 coins
Oil Lamp 5 coins

Meat, Bread, Water, an Oil Lamp

UP CLOSE AND PERSONAL!

Matthew 26:17-30

 **The Challenge**

Number Jesus' disciples alphabetically, and then write the word below each disciple in the matching blank. Read the words in order to discover some good news about Jesus. (Hint: Save the two disciples with the same name for last.)

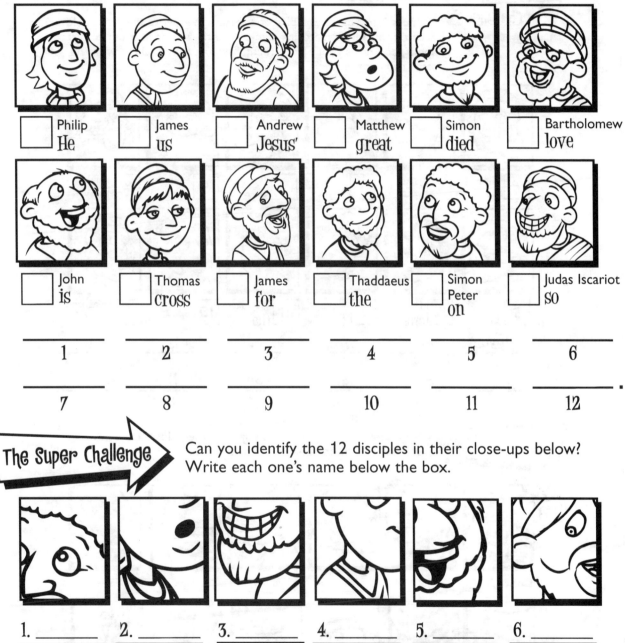

☐ Philip
He

☐ James
us

☐ Andrew
Jesus'

☐ Matthew
great

☐ Simon
died

☐ Bartholomew
love

☐ John
is

☐ Thomas
cross

☐ James
for

☐ Thaddaeus
the

☐ Simon Peter
on

☐ Judas Iscariot
so

___ ___ ___ ___ ___ ___
1   2   3   4   5   6

___ ___ ___ ___ ___ ___ .
7   8   9   10 11 12

The Super Challenge → Can you identify the 12 disciples in their close-ups below? Write each one's name below the box.

1. _____ 2. _____ 3. _____ 4. _____ 5. _____ 6. _____

7. _____ 8. _____ 9. _____ 10. _____ 11. _____ 12. _____

UP CLOSE AND PERSONAL!

Matthew 26:17-30

The Challenge →

Number Jesus' disciples alphabetically, and then write the word below each disciple in the matching blank. Read the words in order to discover some good news about Jesus. (Hint: Save the two disciples with the same name for last.)

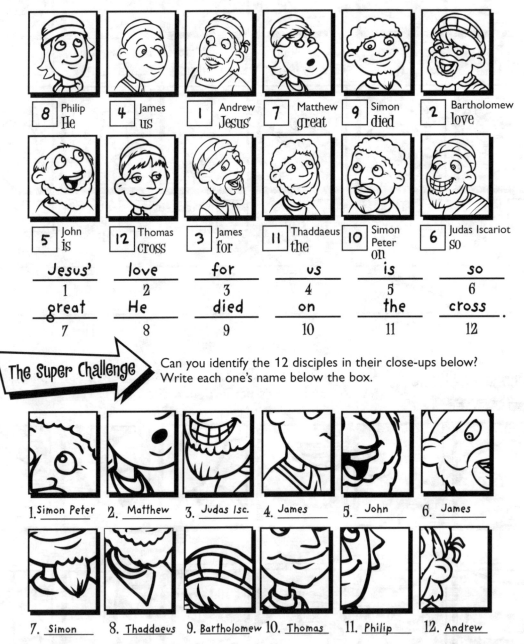

8 Philip	4 James	1 Andrew	7 Matthew	9 Simon	2 Bartholomew
He	us	Jesus'	great	died	love

5 John	12 Thomas	3 James	11 Thaddaeus	10 Simon Peter	6 Judas Iscariot
is	cross	for	the	on	so

Jesus'	love	for	us	is	so
1	2	3	4	5	6

great	He	died	on	the	cross
7	8	9	10	11	12

.

The Super Challenge →

Can you identify the 12 disciples in their close-ups below? Write each one's name below the box.

1. Simon Peter	2. Matthew	3. Judas Isc.	4. James	5. John	6. James

7. Simon	8. Thaddaeus	9. Bartholomew	10. Thomas	11. Philip	12. Andrew

PETER, PETER, HUMBLE PIE EATER!

Matthew 26:31-35,69-75

The Challenge

Jesus loved Peter very much, but that didn't stop Peter from denying his friendship with Jesus. Peter was sorry and wanted to talk to Jesus. Help Peter get to Jesus by following Jesus' special message to Peter: I forgive you. Don't cross over your own path as you go!

Start

Finish

The Super Challenge

Look for eight letters hidden on the sheep, roosters and fish. Unscramble the letters to discover what forgiveness helps us make.

a ___ ___ ___ ___ ___ ___ ___

PETER, PETER, HUMBLE PIE EATER!

Matthew 26:31-35,69-75

The Challenge → Jesus loved Peter very much, but that didn't stop Peter from denying his friendship with Jesus. Peter was sorry and wanted to talk to Jesus. Help Peter get to Jesus by following Jesus' special message to Peter: I forgive you. Don't cross over your own path as you go!

The Super Challenge → Look for eight letters hidden on the sheep, roosters and fish. Unscramble the letters to discover what forgiveness helps us make.

a <u>N E W</u> <u>S T A R T</u>

ON CLOUD NINE!

The Challenge

Matthew 28:16-20

Starting at the letter *I* and finishing at Jesus, go through the maze to find out what Jesus promised before He went to heaven.

The Super Challenge

Find nine letters hidden in the buildings to spell a word that describes when Jesus went to heaven.

On Cloud Nine!

Matthew 28:16-20

The Challenge →

Starting at the letter *I* and finishing at Jesus, go through the maze to find out what Jesus promised before He went to heaven.

I WILL CARE FOR YOU.

The Super Challenge → Find nine letters hidden in the buildings to spell a word that describes when Jesus went to heaven.

A S C E N S I O N

SOW A SEED

Mark 2:1-20

The Challenge Find a message by writing the letters from the seeds in the blanks below.

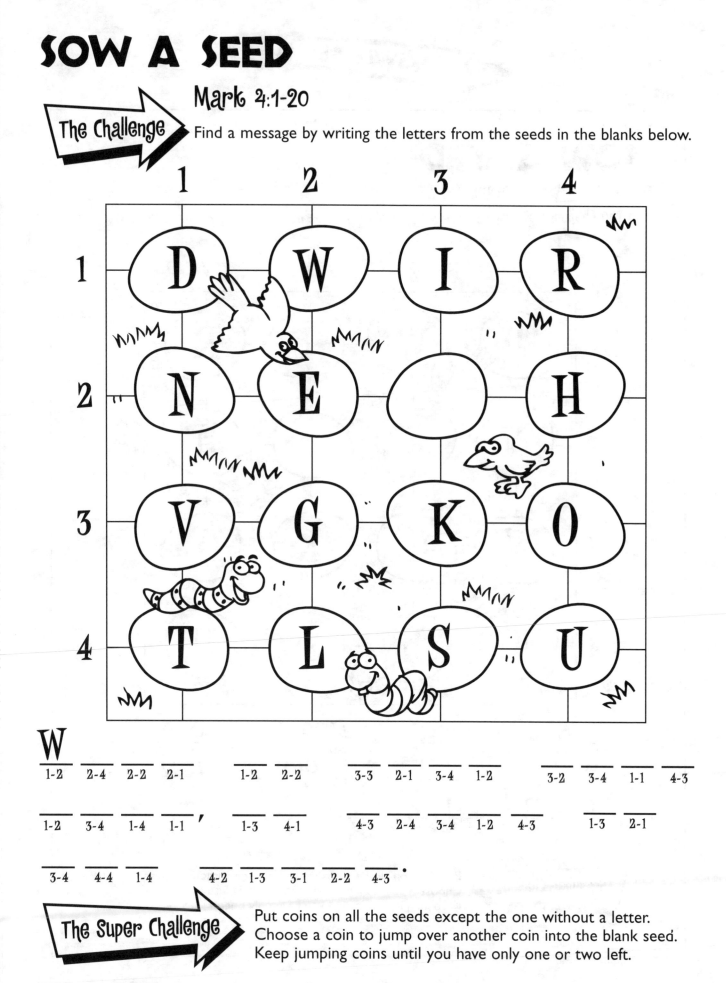

W __ __ __ __   __ __   __ __ __ __   __ __ __ __
1-2 2-4 2-2 2-1   1-2 2-2   3-3 2-1 3-4 1-2   3-2 3-4 1-1 4-3

__ __ __ __ ,   __ __   __ __ __ __ __ __   __ __
1-2 3-4 1-4 1-1   1-3 4-1   4-3 2-4 3-4 1-2 4-3   1-3 2-1

__ __ __   __ __ __ __ __ .
3-4 4-4 1-4   4-2 1-3 3-1 2-2 4-3

The Super Challenge Put coins on all the seeds except the one without a letter. Choose a coin to jump over another coin into the blank seed. Keep jumping coins until you have only one or two left.

SOW A SEED

Mark 4:1-20

The Challenge → Find a message by writing the letters from the seeds in the blanks below.

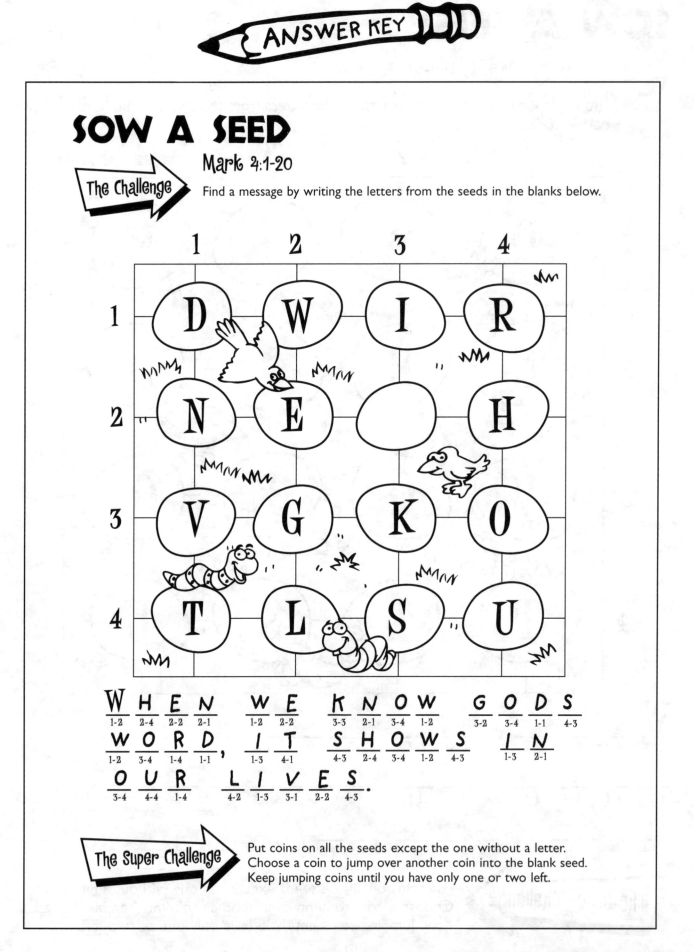

	1	2	3	4
1	D	W	I	R
2	N	E		H
3	V	G	K	O
4	T	L	S	U

W H E N   W E   K N O W   G O D S
1-2 2-4 2-2 2-1   1-2 2-2   3-3 2-1 3-4 1-2   3-2 3-4 1-1 4-3

W O R D,   I T   S H O W S   I N
1-2 3-4 1-4 1-1   1-3 4-1   4-3 2-4 3-4 1-2 4-3   1-3 2-1

O U R   L I V E S.
3-4 4-4 1-4   4-2 1-3 3-1 2-2 4-3

The Super Challenge → Put coins on all the seeds except the one without a letter.
Choose a coin to jump over another coin into the blank seed.
Keep jumping coins until you have only one or two left.

GET A MOVE ON!

The Challenge

Mark 5:21-23

When Jairus's daughter got sick, he asked Jesus for help. Start at the G and go around the circle clockwise, skipping every other letter as you go; go in the opposite direction when you get to the arrow. On the blank lines, write the letters you hit, until you use all the letters. You'll find a way God shows love to us.

_____

The Super Challenge Circle all the things wrong in this picture.

_____ .

GET A MOVE ON!

Mark 5:21-43

The Challenge

When Jairus's daughter got sick, he asked Jesus for help. Start at the *G* and go around the circle clockwise, skipping every other letter as you go; go in the opposite direction when you get to the arrow. On the blank lines, write the letters you hit, until you use all the letters. You'll find a way God shows love to us.

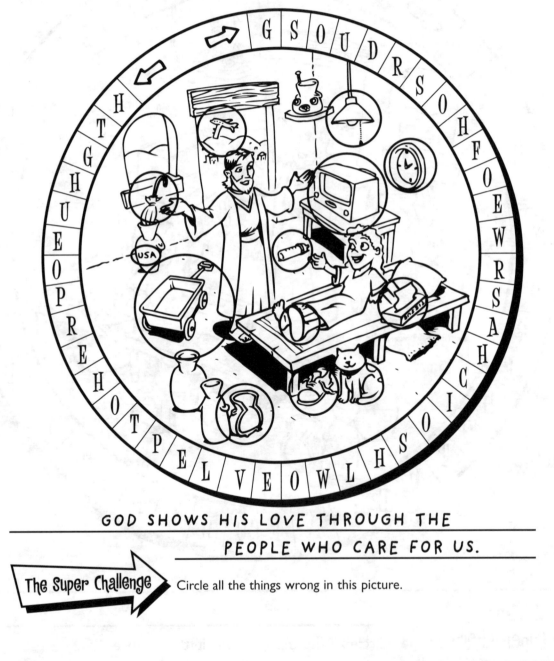

GOD SHOWS HIS LOVE THROUGH THE

PEOPLE WHO CARE FOR US.

The Super Challenge Circle all the things wrong in this picture.

HOSANNA!

The Challenge

Mark 11:1-11

Can you solve the rebus? It's going to echo the shouts of joy that followers of Jesus made when He entered Jerusalem on a donkey.

(hose)-e + (bee)-t (nail)-il

_____

(yo-yo)-al + ES (sled)-L

_____

(fist)-ft (elbow)-el W + (horse)-of

_____

(comet)-t + S (fish)-f (spool)-rad

_____

N (camel)-cl (on/off switch)-f 3-re

_____

L + (sword)-sw.

_____

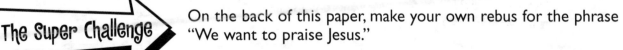

The Super Challenge On the back of this paper, make your own rebus for the phrase "We want to praise Jesus."

HOSANNA!

The Challenge →

Mark 11:1-11

Can you solve the rebus? It's going to echo the shouts of joy that followers of Jesus made when He entered Jerusalem on a donkey.

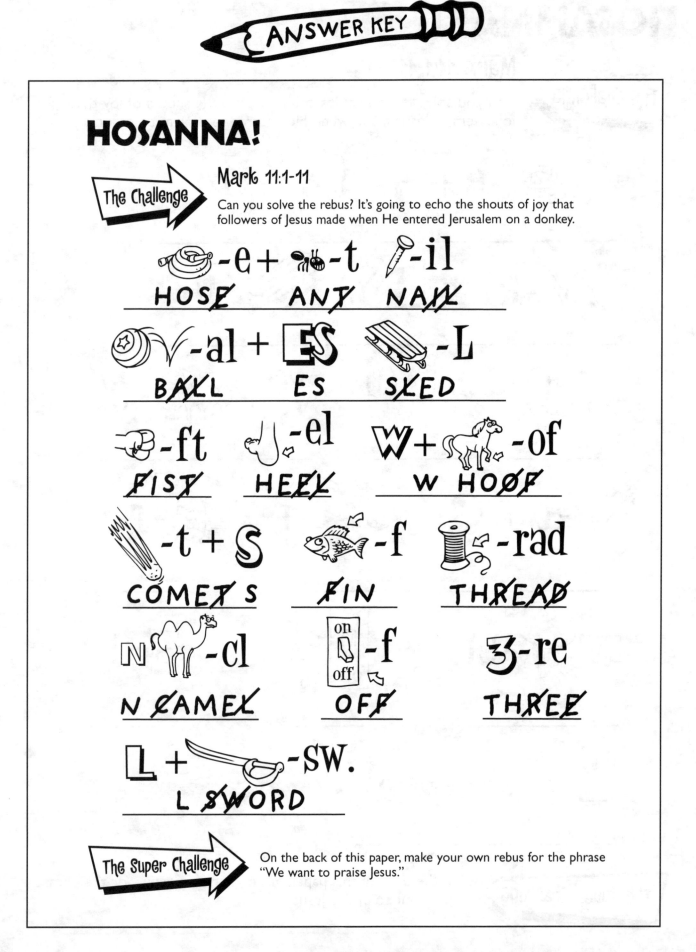

HOSE -e + ANT -t NAIL -il

BALL -al + ES SLED -L

FIST -ft HEEL -el W HOOF + -of

COMET -t + S FIN -f THREAD -rad

N CAMEL -cl OFF -f THREE 3 -re

L + SWORD -sw.

The Super Challenge →

On the back of this paper, make your own rebus for the phrase "We want to praise Jesus."

GOD'S LIFELINE!

Mark 16:1-8

The Challenge → Unscramble the words in the rocks. Write the words in the rectangles according to their numbers. Find the message by reading the rectangles in numerical order.

The Super Challenge → What is the shape that is made when you connect the dots?

_____

GOD'S LIFELINE!

Mark 16:1-8

The Challenge →

Unscramble the words in the rocks. Write the words in the rectangles according to their numbers. Find the message by reading the rectangles in numerical order.

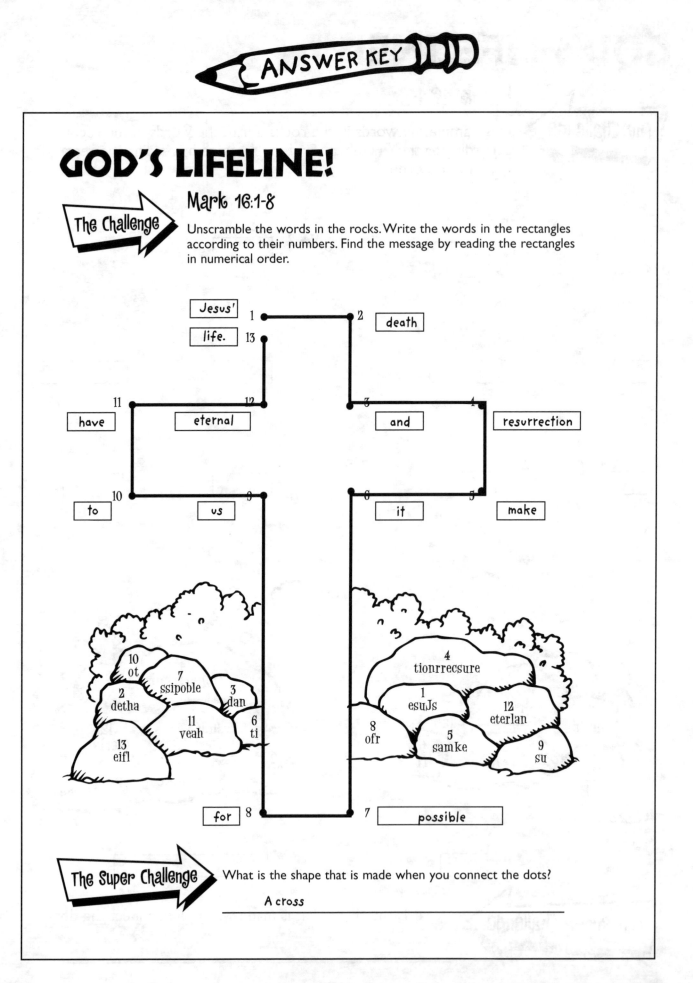

| Jesus' | 1 — 2 | death |
| life. | 13 | |

| have | eternal | 11 — 12 | 3 | and | 4 | resurrection |

| to | us | 10 — 9 | 6 | it | 5 | make |

Rocks:
- 10 ot
- 7 ssipoble
- 2 detha
- 3 dan
- 11 veah
- 6 ti
- 13 eifl
- 4 tionrrecsure
- 1 esuJs
- 12 eterlan
- 8 ofr
- 5 samke
- 9 su

| for | 8 — 7 | possible |

The Super Challenge →

What is the shape that is made when you connect the dots?

A cross

GOING AROUND IN CIRCLES!

Luke 1:26-56

The Challenge

You might get dizzy doing this puzzle! Starting at the letter *F* in the balloon, go clockwise around the circle, skipping a letter each time. Write the letters you land on and you'll discover God's secret message to you, the same message the angel told Mary! Go around the circle twice until every letter is used.

_ _ _ _ _ _ _   _ _ _ _ _ _ _ _ _ _

_ _ _ _ _   _ _ _ _ _ _ _ _ _ _ _ _ _ _

_ _ _ _ _ _ _ _ _ _ _ _ _.

See Luke 1:37.

The Super Challenge Find 10 things in the picture that aren't in the original story of Mary and the angel.

_ _ _ _ _ _ _ _ _ _ _ _ _ _ _ _

_ _ _ _ _ _ _ _ _ _ _ _ _ _ _ _

_ _ _ _ _ _ _ _ _ _ _ _ _ _ _ _

GOING AROUND IN CIRCLES!

Luke 1:26-56

The Challenge →

You might get dizzy doing this puzzle! Starting at the letter *F* in the balloon, go clockwise around the circle, skipping a letter each time. Write the letters you land on and you'll discover God's secret message to you, the same message the angel told Mary! Go around the circle twice until every letter is used.

F O R _ W I T H _ G O D
N O T H I N G _ W I L L _ B E
I M P O S S I B L E.

See Luke 1:37.

The Super Challenge → Find 10 things in the picture that aren't in the original story of Mary and the angel.

BALLOON   SODA CAN   SUITCASE   EYEGLASSES   UMBRELLA

FLAG   CELL PHONE   WATCH   AIRPLANE   SNEAKERS

SUPER STARS!

The Challenge

Luke 2:1-20

The birth of Jesus was heralded in the night sky by the star of Bethlehem. Unscramble the letters in each star cluster to read this celestial message.

The Super Challenge → Circle at least 15 things that are different between each scene.

SUPER STARS!

The Challenge

Luke 2:1-20

The birth of Jesus was heralded in the night sky by the star of Bethlehem. Unscramble the letters in each star cluster to read this celestial message.

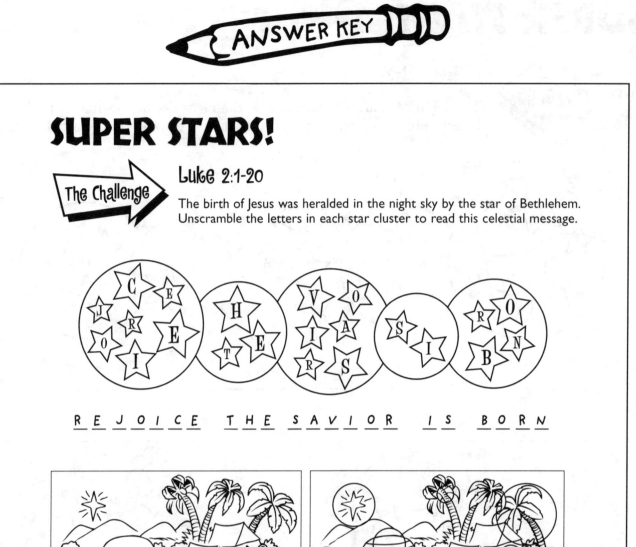

R E J O I C E   T H E   S A V I O R   I S   B O R N

The Super Challenge   Circle at least 15 things that are different between each scene.

20 THINGS ARE DIFFERENT ON THE SECOND SCENE.

LOST AND FOUND

Luke 15:3-7

The Challenge

The shepherd has lost a sheep, and like the Good Shepherd, he will search high and low for it. In the blanks, write the letters you find on the sheep. Read the hints for help. It's a word that tells what God feels for us.

___ ___ ___ ___ ___ ___ ___ ___ ___ ___ ___ ___ ___

(Hints: The first letter is a curve. The sixth and seventh letters are the same consonant. The fourth letter has a straight line and a curve in it. The last letter is a consonant made of three straight lines.)

The Super Challenge

The shepherd is looking for one specific sheep. It looks just like the one in his picture. Can you find it? When you do, circle it.

LOST AND FOUND

Luke 15:3-7

The Challenge

The shepherd has lost a sheep, and like the Good Shepherd, he will search high and low for it. In the blanks, write the letters you find on the sheep. Read the hints for help. It's a word that tells what God feels for us.

C O M P A S S I O N

(Hints: The first letter is a curve. The sixth and seventh letters are the same consonant. The fourth letter has a straight line and a curve in it. The last letter is a consonant made of three straight lines.)

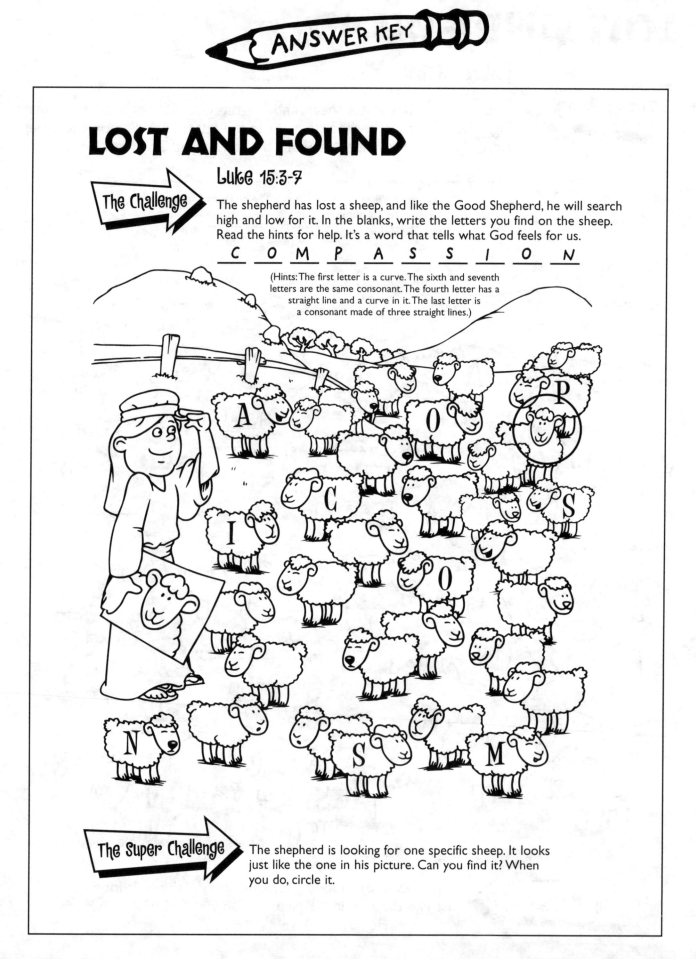

The Super Challenge

The shepherd is looking for one specific sheep. It looks just like the one in his picture. Can you find it? When you do, circle it.

THE HAPPY WANDERER!

Luke 15:11-32

The Challenge

Find the message on the merchant's scroll. Take the first letter from each picture on the scroll and write it on the prodigal son's parchment. Draw lines to divide the letters into words.

BELTS
35 shekels

SANDALS
15 shekels

SCROLLS
70 shekels

RINGS
50 shekels

BREAD
10 shekels

TURBAN
25 shekels

MEAT
60 shekels

ROBES
80 shekels

The Super Challenge

The prodigal son was a happy wanderer for a time. He spent his money foolishly. One day he spent exactly 205 shekels—no more, no less! The five things he bought were all different. Can you figure out what he got for his money?

THE HAPPY WANDERER!

The Challenge

Luke 15:11-32

Find the message on the merchant's scroll. Take the first letter from each picture on the scroll and write it on the prodigal son's parchment. Draw lines to divide the letters into words.

BELTS
35 shekels

SANDALS
15 shekels

SCROLLS
70 shekels

RINGS
50 shekels

BREAD
10 shekels

TURBAN
25 shekels

MEAT
60 shekels

ROBES
80 shekels

GOD WILL

FORGIVE

US WHEN

WE ARE

SORRY

The Super Challenge

The prodigal son was a happy wanderer for a time. He spent his money foolishly. One day he spent exactly 205 shekels—no more, no less! The five things he bought were all different. Can you figure out what he got for his money?

TURBAN   ROBE   SANDALS   BELT   RING

PRAYER PAIR

Luke 18:9-14

The Challenge

A pair of Jews gives us two examples of prayer. One prayer pleases God and one prayer doesn't. Solve the code to discover their prayers.

7 15 4,
20 8 1 14 11
25 15 21
20 8 1 20   9   1 13
2 5 20 20 5 18
20 8 1 14
15 20 8 5 18 19.

7 15 4,
8 1 22 5
13 5 18 3 25
15 14   13 5.
9   1 13   1
19 9 14 14 5 18.

A=1 B=2 C=3
D=4 E=5 F=6
G=7 H=8 I=9
J=10 K=11 L=12
M=13 N=14 O=15
P=16 Q=17 R=18
S=19 T=20 U=21
V=22 W=23
X=24 Y=25 Z=26

First Man's Prayer:

_____

_____

Second Man's Prayer:

_____

_____

The Super Challenge

Unscramble the letters in the pots to make words. Then arrange the words to make a sentence about prayer.

_____ _____ _____ _____ _____.

PRAYER PAIR

Luke 18:9-14

The Challenge

A pair of Jews gives us two examples of prayer. One prayer pleases God and one prayer doesn't. Solve the code to discover their prayers.

7 15 4,
20 8 1 14 11
25 15 21
20 8 1 20 9 1 13
2 5 20 20 5 18
20 8 1 14
15 20 8 5 18 19.

7 15 4,
8 1 22 5
13 5 18 3 25
15 14 13 5.
9 1 13 1
19 9 14 14 5 18.

A=1	B=2	C=3
D=4	E=5	F=6
G=7	H=8	I=9
J=10	K=11	L=12
M=13	N=14	O=15
P=16	Q=17	R=18
S=19	T=20	U=21
	V=22	W=23
X=24	Y=25	Z=26

First Man's Prayer:

GOD, THANK YOU THAT I AM BETTER THAN OTHERS.

Second Man's Prayer:

GOD, HAVE MERCY ON ME. I AM A SINNER.

The Super Challenge

Unscramble the letters in the pots to make words. Then arrange the words to make a sentence about prayer.

Learn   to   pray   from   Jesus'   example .

A TAXING SITUATION!

Luke 19:1-10

The Challenge

Unscramble the letters on Zacchaeus's coins to find a word that tells a way God shows love for us. Write the letters on the blank lines. (Hint: It's something Zacchaeus experienced!)

_____ _____ _____ _____ _____ _____ _____ _____ _____ _____ _____ _____

Breakfast

40 shekels

Lunch

65 shekels

Dinner

_____ shekels

The Super Challenge

Zacchaeus bought 2 goblets of water and a loaf of bread for breakfast. He paid 40 shekels. At lunchtime he bought 3 goblets of water and 2 loaves of bread. Lunch cost him 65 shekels.

How much did a goblet of water cost? _____

How much did he pay for dinner? _____

A TAXING SITUATION!

Luke 19:1-10

The Challenge → Unscramble the letters on Zacchaeus's coins to find a word that tells a way God shows love for us. Write the letters on the blank lines. (Hint: It's something Zacchaeus experienced!)

F O R G I V E N E S S

Breakfast
40 shekels

Lunch
65 shekels

Dinner
120 shekels

The Super Challenge → Zacchaeus bought 2 goblets of water and a loaf of bread for breakfast. He paid 40 shekels. At lunchtime he bought 3 goblets of water and 2 loaves of bread. Lunch cost him 65 shekels.

How much did a goblet of water cost? __15 shekels__

How much did he pay for dinner? __120 shekels__

ACTIONS SPEAK LOUDER THAN WORDS!

The Challenge

John 4:4-42

Collect all the letters of the same style; then unscramble them to form seven words. Arrange them to tell you something great about God.

The Super Challenge

Read what Jesus and the woman at the well said to each other. It should be easy, but if it's not, use a mirror to help you out!

ACTIONS SPEAK LOUDER THAN WORDS!

The Challenge

John 4:4-42

Collect all the letters of the same style; then unscramble them to form seven words. Arrange them to tell you something great about God.

I WHO I SPEAK TO YOU AM THE PROMISED ONE.

I KNOW THE MESSIAH IS COMING. HE WILL TELL US THE TRUTH.

G O D ' S

A C T I O N S

S H O W

H I S

L O V E

F O R   U S .

The Super Challenge

Read what Jesus and the woman at the well said to each other. It should be easy, but if it's not, use a mirror to help you out!

SEEING IS BELIEVING

John 20:19-31

The Challenge ➤ Draw the picture parts in the grid below to see what Thomas saw after Jesus died on the cross. Don't forget to put the letters in for the Super Challenge!

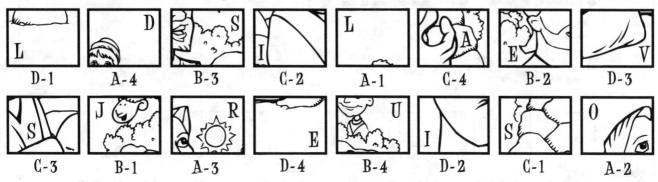

L	D	S		L	A	E	V
D-1	A-4	B-3	C-2	A-1	C-4	B-2	D-3

S	J	R	E	U	I	S	O
C-3	B-1	A-3	D-4	B-4	D-2	C-1	A-2

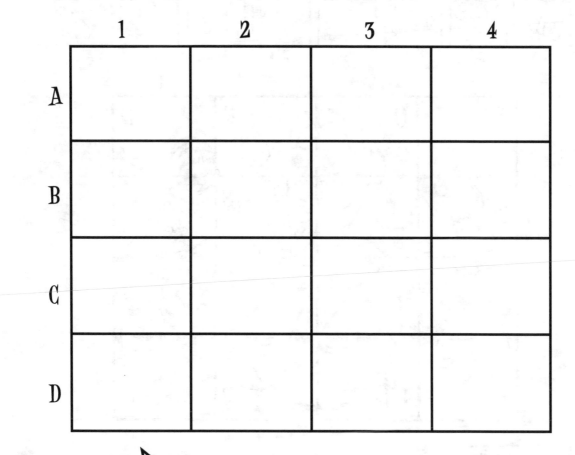

	1	2	3	4
A				
B				
C				
D				

The Super Challenge ➤ Write the letters in order on the blanks below to find out what Thomas might have said after what he saw.

___ ___ ___ ___ ___ ___ ___ ___

___ ___ ___ ___ ___ ___ ___ !

SEEING IS BELIEVING

John 20:19-31

The Challenge → Draw the picture parts in the grid below to see what Thomas saw after Jesus died on the cross. Don't forget to put the letters in for the Super Challenge!

The Super Challenge → Write the letters in order on the blanks below to find out what Thomas might have said after what he saw.

L O R D   J E S U S
I S   A L I V E !

CROWN HIM WITH MANY CROWNS!

The Challenge

Acts 1:4-11

When Jesus returns, the Bible says He will be honored as the King!
Unscramble the letters in each jewel to find 15 names for Jesus, our King.

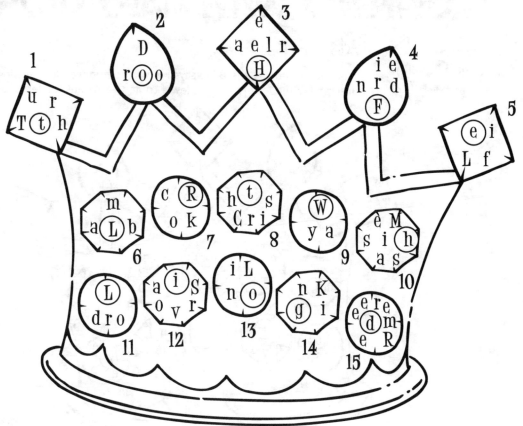

_____

_____

_____

The Super Challenge

Find the circled letter in each jewel and write it on the blank
with the matching number to discover one more name for Jesus!

— — — — —   — —   — — —   — — — — —
6 12 14 10 8   2 4   1 3 5   9 13 7 11 15

CROWN HIM WITH MANY CROWNS!

The Challenge

Acts 1:4-11

When Jesus returns, the Bible says He will be honored as the King!
Unscramble the letters in each jewel to find 15 names for Jesus, our King.

Truth	Door	Healer	Friend	Life
Lamb	Rock	Christ	Way	Messiah
Lord	Savior	Lion	King	Redeemer

The Super Challenge

Find the circled letter in each jewel and write it on the blank
with the matching number to discover one more name for Jesus!

L i g h t   o f   t h e   W o r l d
6 12 14 10 8   2 4   1 3 5   9 13 7 11 15

JESUS—THE GIFTGIVER!

Acts 2:1-21

 The Challenge

Jesus said that after He went to heaven, His Father sent us a special gift. To discover what it was, determine the first letter of each object on the left, follow the path next to each object and put that letter in the box at the end of the path. Read down the column of squares to find out the name of your special gift from Jesus.

 The Super Challenge

Write the words from the squiggles on the line. Then put the words in order to make a sentence about the Holy Spirit.

_____

_____

JESUS—THE GIFTGIVER!

Acts 2

The Challenge → Jesus said that after He went to heaven, His Father sent us a special gift. To discover what it was, determine the first letter of each object on the left, follow the path next to each object and put that letter in the box at the end of the path. Read down the column of squares to find out the name of your special gift from Jesus.

The Super Challenge → Write the words from the squiggles on the line. Then put the words in order to make a sentence about the Holy Spirit.

way helps God's Holy to live Spirit us The

The Holy Spirit helps us to live God's way.

FIRST CHURCH SEARCH

Acts 2:42-47

The Challenge ➤ The early Church showed love and obedience for God in lots of ways. In the puzzle below, find some words that describe the attitudes and actions of the first Christians.

believers
blessing
caring
faithful
fellowship
forgiven
giving
glad
grateful
happy
helping
hopeful
humble
joyful
loving
obedient
praise
prayer
preaching
saved
sharing
singing
teaching
witnessing
worship

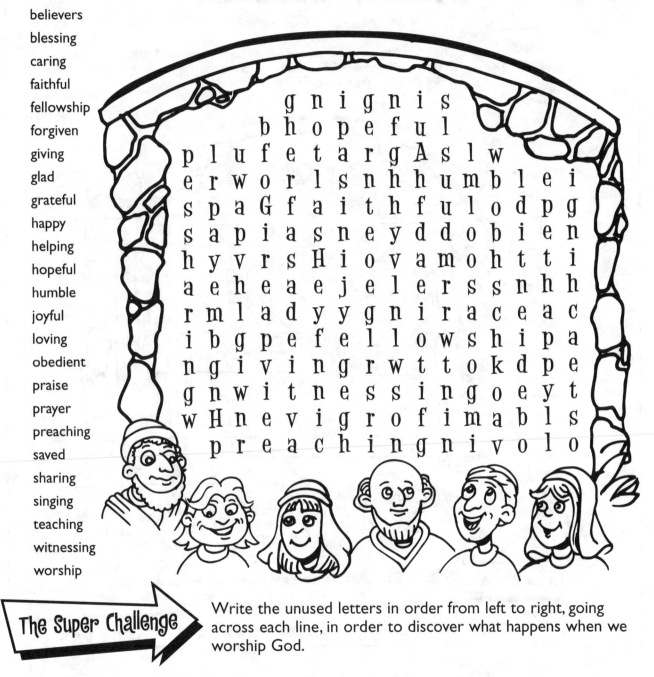

The Super Challenge ➤ Write the unused letters in order from left to right, going across each line, in order to discover what happens when we worship God.

_____

_____

_____

FIRST CHURCH SEARCH

Acts 2:42-47

The Challenge

The early Church showed love and obedience for God in lots of ways. In the puzzle below, find some words that describe the attitudes and actions of the first Christians.

believers
blessing
caring
faithful
fellowship
forgiven
giving
glad
grateful
happy
helping
hopeful
humble
joyful
loving
obedient
praise
prayer
preaching
saved
sharing
singing
teaching
witnessing
worship

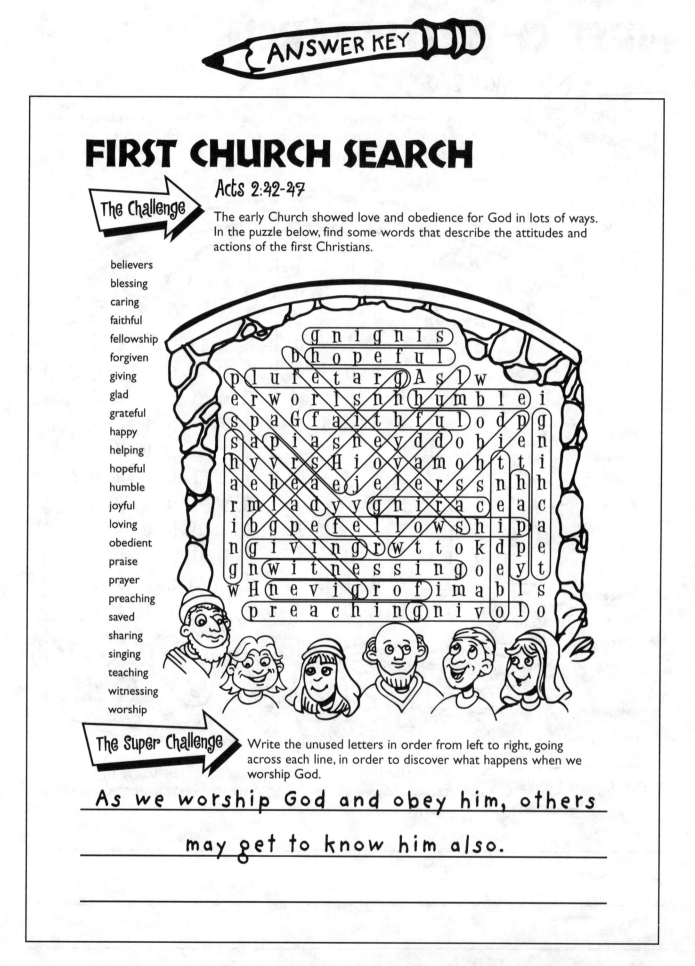

The Super Challenge

Write the unused letters in order from left to right, going across each line, in order to discover what happens when we worship God.

As we worship God and obey him, others

may get to know him also.

STEPHEN WAS NO LOAFER!

Acts 6:1-7

The Challenge

Unscramble the words to find a special message about Stephen, one of God's most faithful followers.

_____ _____ _ ____
pnetShe   swa   a   nam

__ _____.
fo   aifht

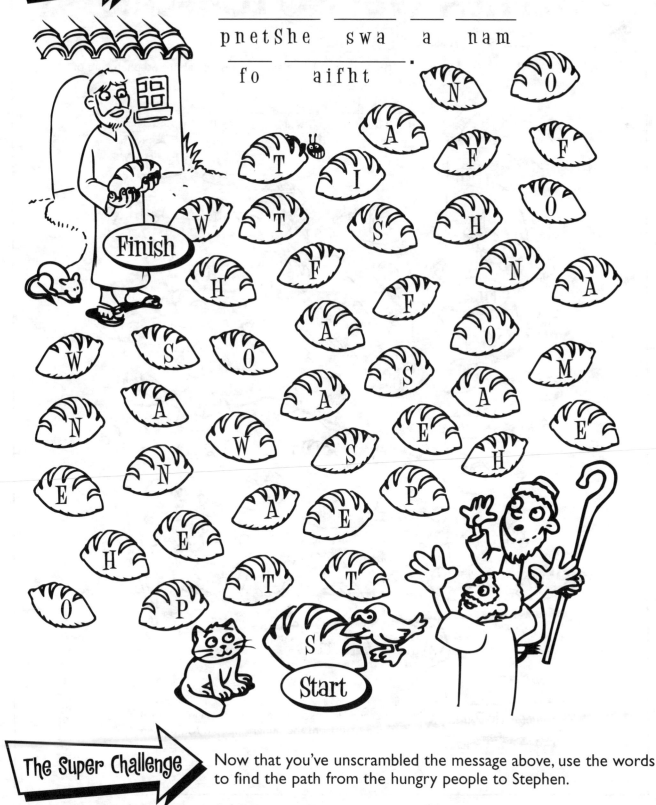

The Super Challenge

Now that you've unscrambled the message above, use the words to find the path from the hungry people to Stephen.

STEPHEN WAS NO LOAFER!

Acts 6:1-7

The Challenge

Unscramble the words to find a special message about Stephen, one of God's most faithful followers.

Stephen	was	a	man
pnetShe	swa	a	nam

of	faith
fo	aifht

Finish

Start

The Super Challenge

Now that you've unscrambled the message above, use the words to find the path from the hungry people to Stephen.

SEEK AND YE SHALL FIND!

Acts 8:26-40

The Challenge

Philip is on his way to the Ethiopian man, but Philip is not sure where to look. See if you can help him. Trace his path from dot to dot so you can do the Super Challenge.

1. Start at the building that is 1 inch tall.
2. Go to the nearest palm tree.
3. Count the rocks under it. Go west that many inches. Then go south.
4. When you reach a tent, go east 2½ inches.
5. At the cave, turn and go north until you reach a building.
6. Go to the nearest sheep.
7. Head southwest 3 inches.
8. Congratulations! You've found the Ethiopian! Where is he?

_____

The Super Challenge

If you found the Ethiopian correctly, write the letters next to the landmarks as you went and you'll discover what Phillip told the Ethiopian about Jesus. __ __ __ __ __ __ __ __

SEEK AND YE SHALL FIND!

Acts 8:26-40

The Challenge

Philip is on his way to the Ethiopian man, but Philip is not sure where to look. See if you can help him. Trace his path from dot to dot so you can do the Super Challenge.

1. Start at the building that is 1 inch tall.
2. Go to the nearest palm tree.
3. Count the rocks under it. Go west that many inches. Then go south.
4. When you reach a tent, go east 2½ inches.
5. At the cave, turn and go north until you reach a building.

6. Go to the nearest sheep.
7. Head southwest 3 inches.
8. Congratulations! You've found the Ethiopian! Where is he?

AT THE TWIN PALM TREES

The Super Challenge

If you found the Ethiopian correctly, write the letters next to the landmarks as you went and you'll discover what Phillip told the Ethiopian about Jesus. G O O D   N E W S

ROADWORTHY

Acts 9:1-31

The Challenge

Before Saul* believed in Jesus, Saul's job was to find Christians and put them in prison. All that changed when he met Jesus on the road to Damascus. Can you work out the message Jesus gave Saul by unscrambling the words in the burst?

JESUS' MESSAGE:_____

_____

The Super Challenge

Find the squares above in the grid. Be careful; some of them have been turned upside down! Use the numbers and letters to write the coordinates.

* Saul's name was later changed to Paul.

111

ROADWORTHY

Acts 9:1-31

The Challenge → Before Saul* believed in Jesus, Saul's job was to find Christians and put them in prison. All that changed when he met Jesus on the road to Damascus. Can you work out the message Jesus gave Saul by unscrambling the words in the burst?

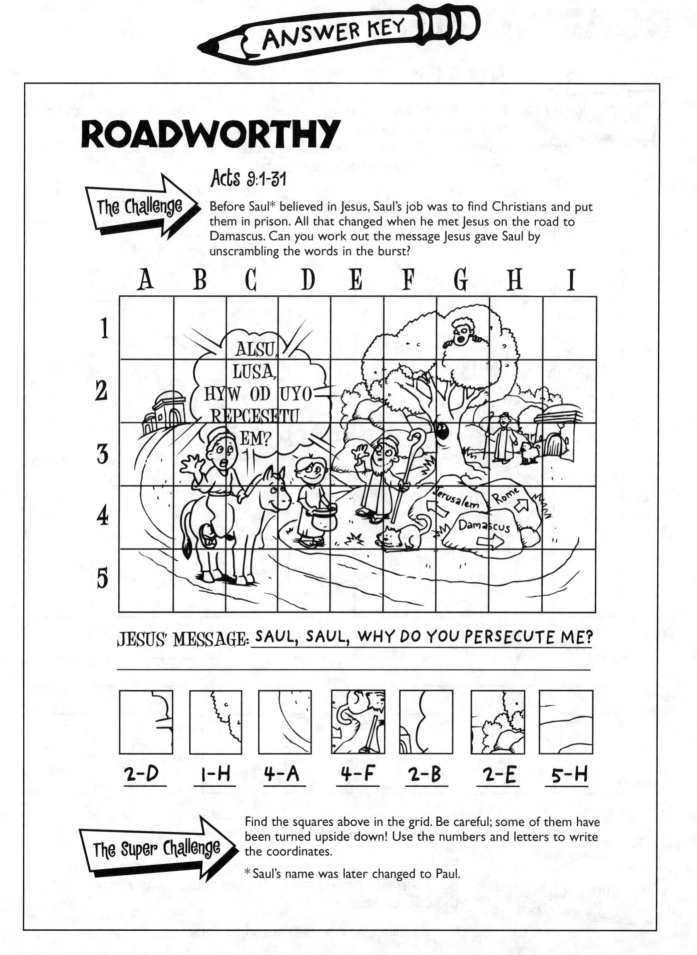

A B C D E F G H I

1 2 3 4 5

In the burst: ALSU, LUSA, HYW OD UYO REPCESETU EM?

JESUS' MESSAGE: SAUL, SAUL, WHY DO YOU PERSECUTE ME?

2-D   1-H   4-A   4-F   2-B   2-E   5-H

The Super Challenge → Find the squares above in the grid. Be careful; some of them have been turned upside down! Use the numbers and letters to write the coordinates.

*Saul's name was later changed to Paul.

TAKE NOTE!

Exodus 15:2

The Challenge → Make a joyful noise to the Lord! For this puzzle, you have to be able to read music (sort of!). Use the music-note code to write out the verse that will be music to your ears!

TAKE NOTE!

Exodus 15:2

The Challenge

Make a joyful noise to the Lord! For this puzzle, you have to be able to read music(sort of!). Use the music-note code to write out the verse that will be music to your ears!

"THE LORD IS MY STRENGTH AND MY SONG; HE HAS BECOME MY SALVA- TION. HE IS MY GOD, AND I WILL PRAISE HIM."

BREAKING UP IS HARD TO DO!

The Challenge

Exodus 20:8

Oops! The cat accidently knocked over Mom's favorite plate. Can you uncover today's Bible verse by putting the plate back together? Write the letters in the correct spaces.

BREAKING UP IS HARD TO DO!

The Challenge →

Exodus 20:8

Oops! The cat accidently knocked over Mom's favorite plate. Can you uncover today's Bible verse by putting the plate back together? Write the letters in the correct spaces.

bb
by
k
mb
er
at
ho

Remember
the Sabbath
day by
keeping
it holy.

t
g
ly.
eep
in
Sa
d
h
me
he
Re
it
ay

DEAR DIARY!

The Challenge ➡

Joshua 1:9

Number each word on the diary page (Dear = 1, God = 2, and so on) till you reach the end of the page. Then fill in the numbered blanks at the bottom with the matching words to find a special Bible verse for you.

Dear God,

I am going to the dentist today and I'll try to be brave, but you know I'm not very courageous. Please do not be discouraged with me. Lord, you know I will try hard to be strong and with your help, I will be! I know you are concerned for me and look after me wherever I go. You are the most awesome God!

"

_____ _____ _____
  26   39   54

_____ •••• _____ _____
        22   24   20

____ _____ ,
 14   27

_____ _____ _____ _____
 52   63   30   42

_____ _____ _____ _____
 66   34   46   41

_____ _____ _____ _____ _____ .
 49   58   17   60   "

DEAR DIARY!

Joshua 1:9

The Challenge ➜ Number each word on the diary page (Dear = 1, God = 2, and so on) till you reach the end of the page. Then fill in the numbered blanks at the bottom with the matching words to find a special Bible verse for you.

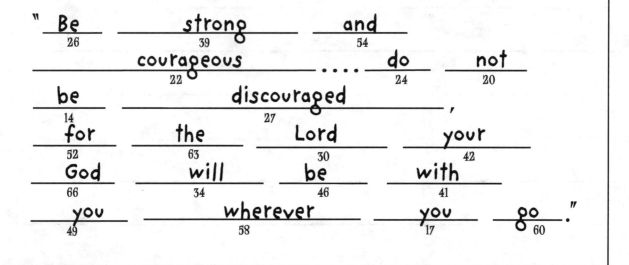

Dear God,

I am going to the dentist today and I'll try to be brave, but you know I'm not very courageous. Please do not be discouraged with me. Lord, you know I will try hard to be strong and with your help, I will be! I know you are concerned for me and look after me wherever I go. You are the most awesome God!

" Be   strong   and
  26   39   54

    courageous .... do   not
        22   24   20

be   discouraged   ,
14   27

for   the   Lord   your
52   63   30   42

God   will   be   with
66   34   46   41

you   wherever   you   go ."
49   58   17   60

PINBALL PARLOR!

The Challenge

1 Chronicles 16:29

"Ascribe to the Lord the glory due his name. Bring an offering and come before him; worship the Lord."

Follow the arrows to find the path that goes through all the words of the verse.

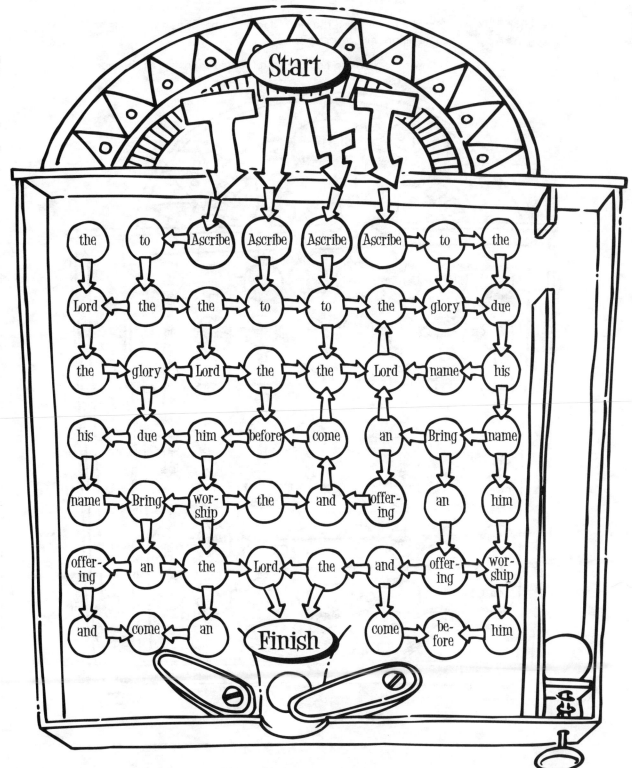

PINBALL PARLOR!

1 Chronicles 16:29

The Challenge → "Ascribe to the Lord the glory due his name. Bring an offering and come before him; worship the Lord."

Follow the arrows to find the path that goes through all the words of the verse.

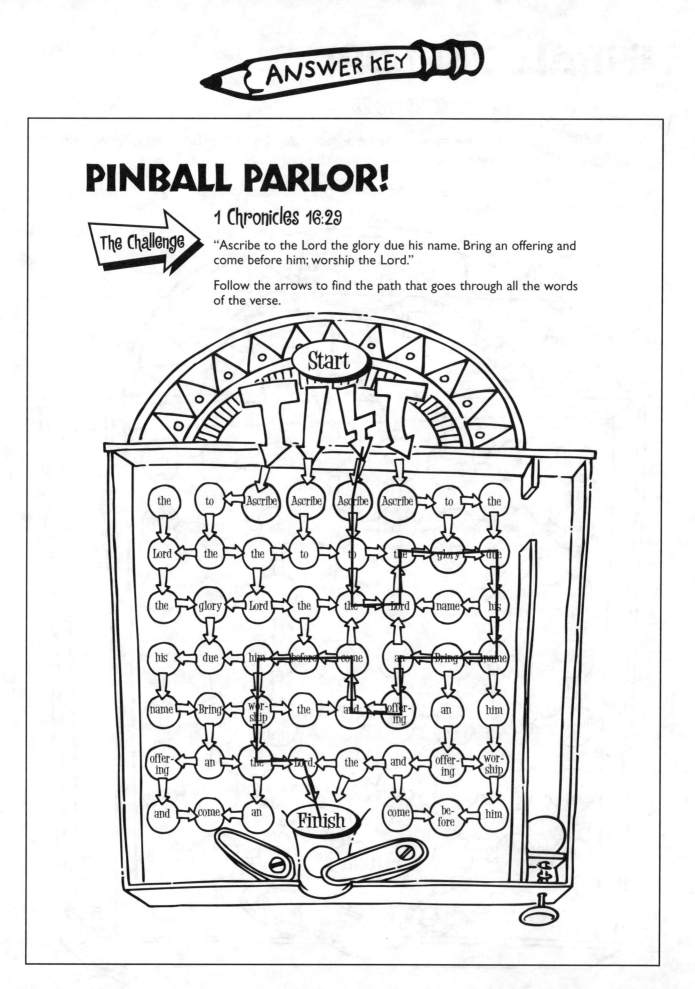

WALL TO WALL SCRIPTURE

Psalm 18:2

The Challenge → The bricklayer's been busy—and a little careless. He didn't lay the bricks in order. Find the numbered blank each brick matches. Write the words in the blanks to read the verse.

29 my   13 is   24 shield

4 my   15 rock   12 God   16 in   21 He

26 the   25 and   3 is   30 salvation   8 and

19 take   7 fortress   17 whom   2 Lord   20 refuge

32 stronghold   11 my   1 The   22 is

31 my   27 horn   23 my   28 of   6 my

14 my   18 I   9 my   5 rock   10 deliverer

" The ___ ___ ___ ___ ___ , ___ ___ ___
   1   2   3   4   5   6   7   8

___ ___ ; ___ ___ ___ ___ ___ , ___
  9   10   11   12   13   14   15   16

___ ___ ___ ___ . ___ ___ ___ ___
  17   18   19   20   21   22   23   24

___ ___ ___ ___ ___ ___ , ___ ___ . "
  25   26   27   28   29   30   31   32

WALL TO WALL SCRIPTURE

Psalm 18:2

The Challenge → The bricklayer's been busy—and a little careless. He didn't lay the bricks in order. Find the numbered blank each brick matches. Write the words in the blanks to read the verse.

29 my	13 is	24 shield

4 my	15 rock	12 God	16 in	21 He
26 the	25 and	3 is	30 salvation	8 and
19 take	7 fortress	17 whom	2 Lord	20 refuge
32 stronghold		11 my	1 The	22 is
31 my	27 horn	23 my	28 of	6 my
14 my	18 I	9 my	5 rock	10 deliverer

"The Lord is my rock, my fortress and
  1   2   3   4   5   6   7   8

my deliverer; my God is my rock, in
 9   10   11 12 13 14 15   16

whom I take refuge. He is my shield
 17 18 19   20   21 22 23   24

and the horn of my salvation, my stronghold."
 25   26   27 28 29   30   31   32

Psalm 32:8

The Challenge Become the teacher's pet by breaking the code. Use the key above the blackboard to go to the top of the class!

Code: GVLOINSEYTAWPJXBUZDRFKCMQH
Real: ABCDEFGHIJKLMNOPQRSTUVWXYZ

"Y CYWW YJDRZFLR QXF
_____

GJO RIGLE QXF YJ REI
_____

CGQ QXF DEXFWO SX Y
_____;

CYWW LXFJDIW QXF GJO
_____

CGRLE XKIZ QXF
_____."

TEACHER'S PET!

Psalm 32:8

The Challenge

Become the teacher's pet by breaking the code. Use the key above the blackboard to go to the top of the class!

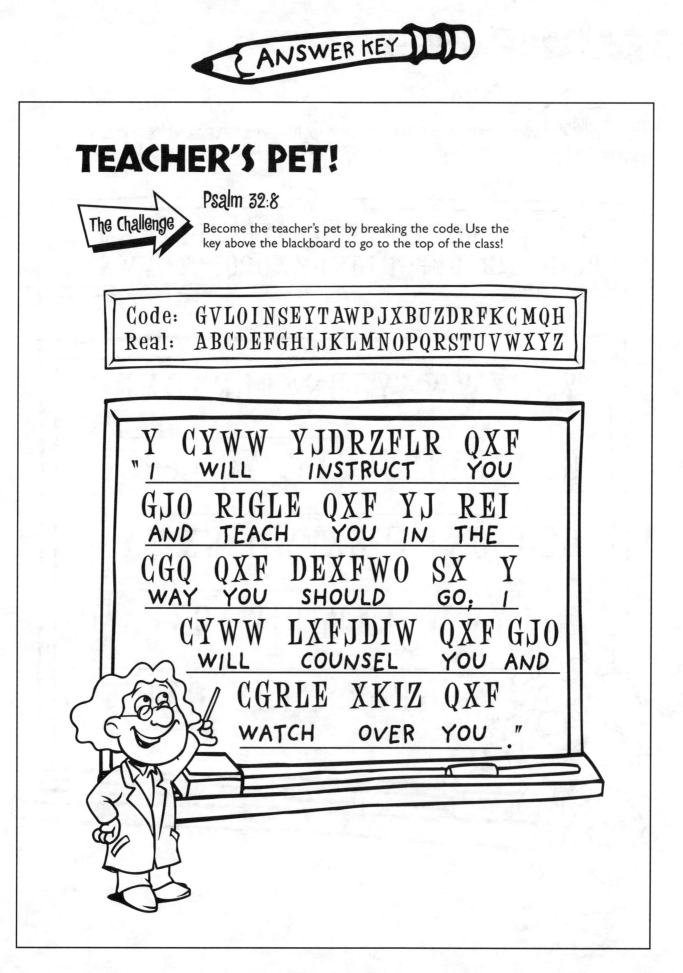

Code: G V L O I N S E Y T A W P J X B U Z D R F K C M Q H
Real: A B C D E F G H I J K L M N O P Q R S T U V W X Y Z

Y CYWW YJDRZFLR QXF
" I WILL INSTRUCT YOU

GJO RIGLE QXF YJ REI
AND TEACH YOU IN THE

CGQ QXF DEXFWO SX Y
WAY YOU SHOULD GO, I

CYWW LXFJDIW QXF GJO
WILL COUNSEL YOU AND

CGRLE XKIZ QXF
WATCH OVER YOU ."

MUSIC TO YOUR EARS!

Psalm 33:11

The word of God is music to your ears. If you follow the instructions, you'll have something to sing about.

Step 1: Cross off the jobs.

Step 2: Cross out all the words with a double *z* in them.

Step 3: Everyone loves animals, but we don't need them here.

Step 4: You didn't eat your vegetables, so cross off all the desserts!

Step 5: Cross off the places to go.

Step 6: Finally, lose all the round things.

Step 7: Write the remaining words on the blank lines.

mouse	The	artist	beach	plans
of	ring	the	pudding	ice cream
fizzy	Lord	muzzle	stand	moon
firm	movies	duck	kangaroo	forever
cake	the	wheel	purposes	jazz
of	gardener	his	mall	bubble
ball	heart	pie	cat	through
all	park	generations	teacher	vet

MUSIC TO YOUR EARS!

Psalm 33:11

The Challenge ➤ The word of God is music to your ears. If you follow the instructions, you'll have something to sing about.

Step 1: Cross off the jobs.

Step 2: Cross out all the words with a double *z* in them.

Step 3: Everyone loves animals, but we don't need them here.

Step 4: You didn't eat your vegetables, so cross off all the desserts!

Step 5: Cross off the places to go.

Step 6: Finally, lose all the round things.

Step 7: Write the remaining words on the blank lines.

mouse	The	artist	beach	plans
of	ring	the	pudding	ice cream
fizzy	Lord	muzzle	stand	moon
firm	movies	duck	kangaroo	forever
cake	the	wheel	purposes	jazz
of	gardener	his	mall	bubble
ball	heart	pie	cat	through
all	park	generations	teacher	vet

" The plans of the Lord
stand firm forever the purposes
of his heart through all
generations "

SLAM DUNK!

The Challenge

Psalm 46:1

Write the letters in the spaces of the net, following the direction of the arrows. If the arrow goes up, write the letters from the bottom to the top in order. If the arrow goes down, write the letters from the top to the bottom in order. The first one is done for you. Then read the Bible verse.

SLAM DUNK!

Psalm 46:1

The Challenge

Write the letters in the spaces of the net, following the direction of the arrows. If the arrow goes up, write the letters from the bottom to the top in order. If the arrow goes down, write the letters from the top to the bottom in order. The first one is done for you. Then read the Bible verse.

© 2000 by Gospel Light. Permission to photocopy granted. *The Big Book of Bible Puzzles*

YOU'VE GOT MAIL!

Psalm 67:1,2

The Challenge — The mailman has a special message hidden in the mail delivery for you. The postage is the clue. Fill in the blanks from the lowest postage to the highest to find the Bible message.

among all	85
upon us	55
ways may	65
that your	60
be known	70
to us	30
us and	40
on earth	75
face shine	50
May God	20
nations	90
be gracious	25
make his	45
and bless	35
your salvation	80

"___ ___ ___ ___ ___ ___ ___ ___

___ ___ ___ ___ ___ ___ ___

___ ___ ___ ___ , ___ ___ ___

___ ___ ___ ___ ___ ___ ___ ,

___ ___ ___ ___ ___ ."

YOU'VE GOT MAIL!

Psalm 67:1,2

The Challenge ➤ The mailman has a special message hidden in the mail delivery for you. The postage is the clue. Fill in the blanks from the lowest postage to the highest to find the Bible message.

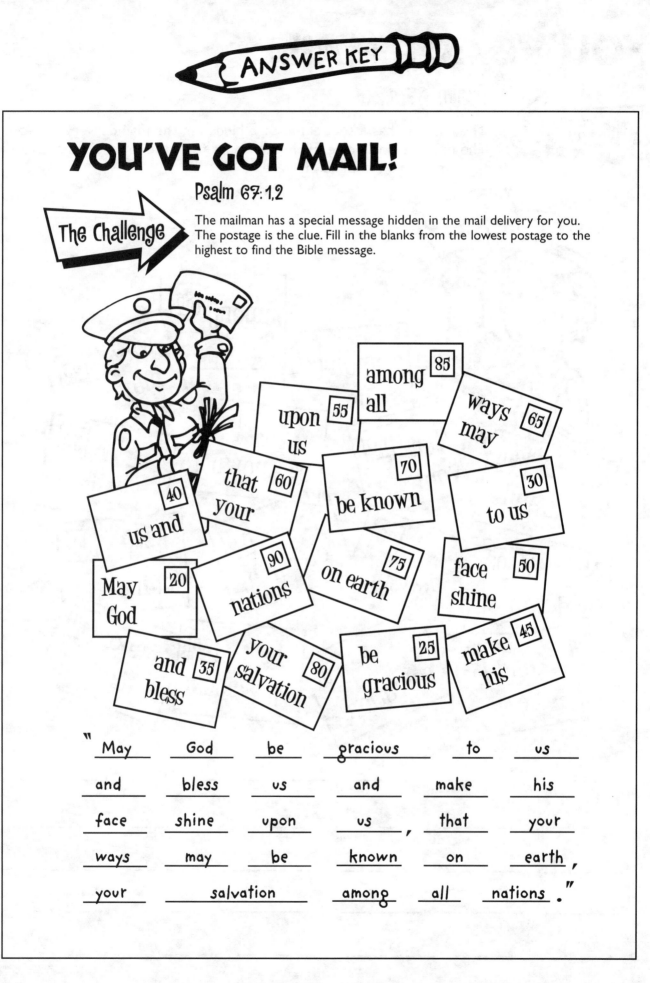

among all [85]

upon us [55]

ways may [65]

that your [60]

be known [70]

to us [30]

us and [40]

May God [20]

nations [90]

on earth [75]

face shine [50]

and bless [35]

your salvation [80]

be gracious [25]

make his [45]

" May   God   be   gracious   to   us

and   bless   us   and   make   his

face   shine   upon   us ,   that   your

ways   may   be   known   on   earth ,

your   salvation   among   all   nations ."

HIP HOP

Psalm 69:13

Hey, this hip frog thinks he's cool enough to hop alphabetically from lily-pad to lilypad to find a really mixed up Bible verse. Betcha won't croak if you try it, too!

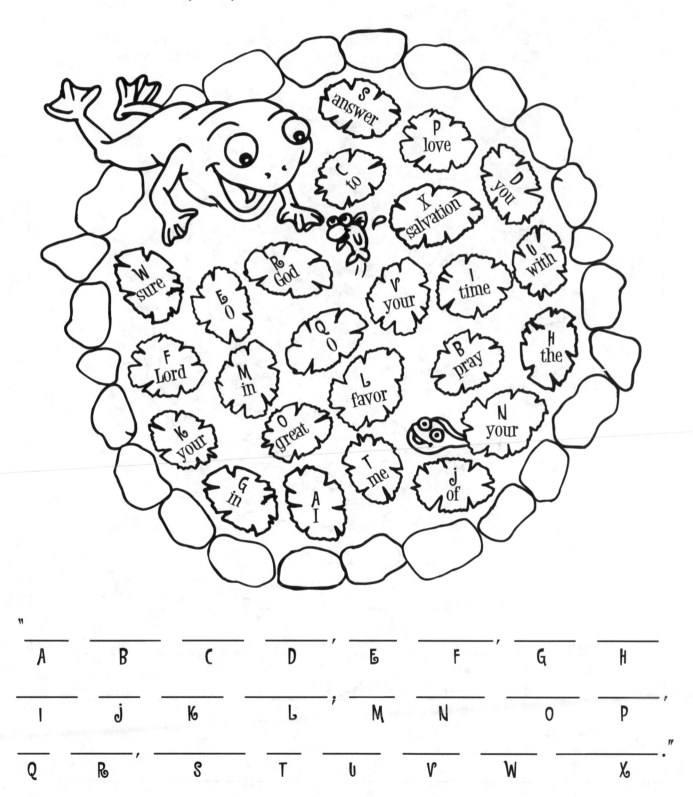

" ___ ___ ___ ___ ___ ' ___ ___ ___ ,
A   B   C   D   E   F   G   H

___ ___ ___ ___ ___ ; ___ ___ ___ ___ ,
I   J   K   L   M   N   O   P

___ ___ , ___ ___ ___ ___ ___ ___ . "
Q   R   S   T   U   V   W   X

HIP HOP

The Challenge →

Psalm 69:13

Hey, this hip frog thinks he's cool enough to hop alphabetically from lily-pad to lilypad to find a really mixed up Bible verse. Betcha won't croak if you try it, too!

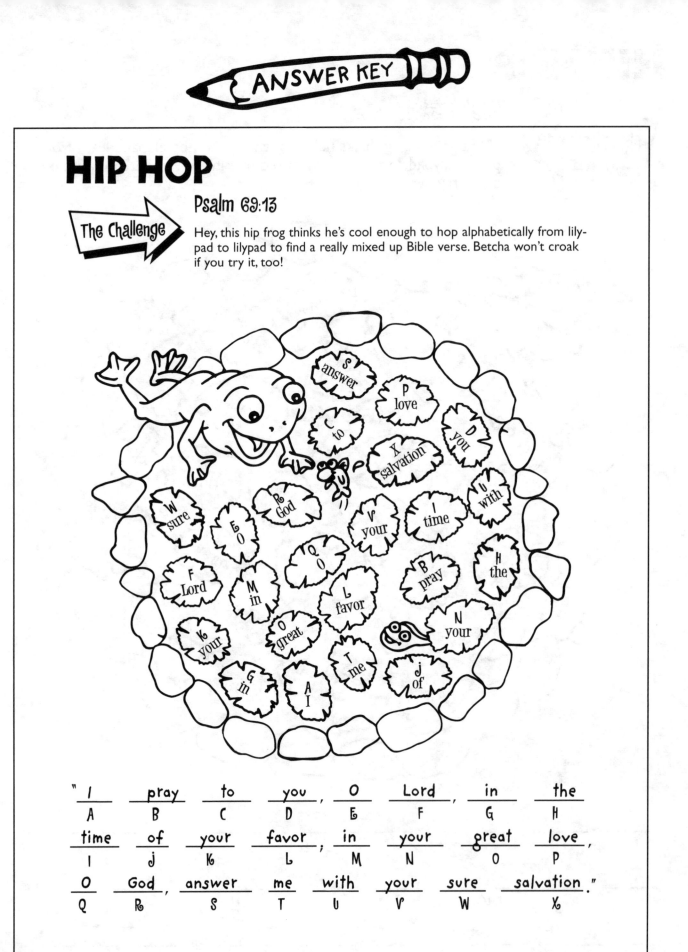

" I	pray	to	you	, O	Lord	, in	the
A	B	C	D	E	F	G	H

time	of	your	favor	, in	your	great	love
I	J	K	L	M	N	O	P

, O	God	, answer	me	with	your	sure	salvation . "
Q	R	S	T	U	V	W	X

BREAKER-BREAKER!

Psalm 77:12

The Challenge → Break the code using the kids' code books to reveal the Bible verse.

For example: B O Y

For example: G I R L

"___ ___ ___

___ ___ ___ ___

___

___ ___ ___ ___

."

BREAKER-BREAKER!

Psalm 77:12

The Challenge Break the code using the kids' code books to reveal the Bible verse.

For example:
B O Y

For example:
G I R L

"I will meditate

on all your works

and consider

all your mighty

deeds."

JUST MY TYPE!

Psalm 100:3

The Challenge ➤ This guy needs to practice his typing a bit more. Each underlined letter should have been substituted for the previous letter in the alphabet. So instead of typing the letter *A* he typed *B*, and instead of *B*, he typed *C*. Help him write out Psalm 100:3 correctly, so he can memorize it!

"Lnox thau uhe More
_____

it Hod. Iu it hf whp
_____

naee vs, ane xe
_____

arf iis."
_____

JUST MY TYPE!

Psalm 100:3

The Challenge This guy needs to practice his typing a bit more. Each underlined letter should have been substituted for the previous letter in the alphabet. So instead of typing the letter *A* he typed *B*, and instead of *B*, he typed *C*. Help him write out Psalm 100:3 correctly, so he can memorize it!

"L̲nox̲ tha̲u u̲he M̲ore̲
Know   that   the   Lord

it̲ H̲od. Iu̲ it̲ hf̲ whp̲
is God. It is   he   who

n̲ae̲e v̲s, ane̲ x̲e
made   us,   and   we

arf̲ ii̲s."
are his.

THEY'RE PLAYING OUR SONG!

Psalm 105:2

The Challenge → Unscramble all the words in the maze. Then trace a path through the maze. When you get to the end, you'll discover what the kids are singing about.

Start

lal _____

ot _____

ngiS _____

gins _____

aisepr _____

odG _____

imh _____

ot _____

imh _____

Finish

mhi _____

ngiS _____

derfulwon _____

tcas _____.

letl _____

ot _____

ctsa _____.

lal _____

fo _____

fo _____

ihs _____

THEY'RE PLAYING OUR SONG!

Psalm 105:2

The Challenge → Unscramble all the words in the maze. Then trace a path through the maze. When you get to the end, you'll discover what the kids are singing about.

Start

lal _all_

ot _to_

ngiS _sing_

aisepr _praise_

odG _God_

imh _him_

gins _sing_

imh _him_

ot _to_

darfulwon _wonderful_

ngiS _sing_

Finish

mht _him_

letl _tell_

tcas _acts._

ot _to_

ctsa _acts._

lal _all_

ihs _his_

fo _of_

fo _of_

LIBRARY LOONIES!

Psalm 119:11

The Challenge ➤ There are some very loony books at the library these days. Put the books in alphabetical order. (Hint: Number them in the circles on the spines.) Take the middle word from each title and write the words in order below to read the verse.

" ___ ___ ___ ___

___ ___ ___ ___ ___ ___ ___ ___ ___ ___ . "

LIBRARY LOONIES!

Psalm 119:11

 The Challenge

There are some very loony books at the library these days. Put the books in alphabetical order. (Hint: Number them in the circles on the spines.) Take the middle word from each title and write the words in order below to read the verse.

" <u>I</u> <u>have</u> <u>hidden</u> <u>your</u> <u>word</u> <u>in</u> <u>my</u> <u>heart</u> <u>that</u> <u>I</u> <u>might</u> <u>not</u> <u>sin</u> <u>against</u> <u>you</u>. "

BOOK 'EM

Psalm 119:66

"Teach me knowledge and good judgment, for I believe in your commands."

Use the words of the verse to get from start to finish. Don't jump over any book or cross over any book. It can be tricky because the words are repeated on more than one book.

BOOK 'EM

Psalm 119:66

"Teach me knowledge and good judgment, for I believe in your commands."

The Challenge

Use the words of the verse to get from start to finish. Don't jump over any book or cross over any book. It can be tricky because the words are repeated on more than one book.

IT'S IN THE BAG!

Psalm 136:1

The Challenge →

The answer to this puzzle is in the suitcase. Fill in the blanks in each sentence. Use the numbers under each answer to fill in the puzzle on the suitcase. You'll find a verse that tells what we can do.

1. Don't slam the __ __ __ __ .
             1 2 3 4

2. You are a __ __ __ __ __ being.
          5 6 7 8 9

3. Birds fly using their __ __ __ __ __ .
        10 11 12 13 14

4. You can watch cartoons on __ __ .
             15 16

5. The tiniest piece of snow is called a snow __ __ __ __ __ .
       17 18 19 20 21

IT'S IN THE BAG!

Psalm 136:1

The Challenge ➤ The answer to this puzzle is in the suitcase. Fill in the blanks in each sentence. Use the numbers under each answer to fill in the puzzle on the suitcase. You'll find a verse that tells what we can do.

1. Don't slam the $\underset{1}{D}$ $\underset{2}{O}$ $\underset{3}{O}$ $\underset{4}{R}$.

2. You are a $\underset{5}{H}$ $\underset{6}{U}$ $\underset{7}{M}$ $\underset{8}{A}$ $\underset{9}{N}$ being.

3. Birds fly using their $\underset{10}{W}$ $\underset{11}{I}$ $\underset{12}{N}$ $\underset{13}{G}$ $\underset{14}{S}$.

4. You can watch cartoons on $\underset{15}{T}$ $\underset{16}{V}$.

5. The tiniest piece of snow is called a snow $\underset{17}{F}$ $\underset{18}{L}$ $\underset{19}{A}$ $\underset{20}{K}$ $\underset{21}{E}$.

"GIVE THANKS TO THE LORD, FOR HE IS GOOD. HIS LOVE ENDURES FOREVER."

THE PAPER ROUTE

Psalm 147:1

This boy is delivering his papers. Go in the direction of the arrows to spell out the verse. Watch out for one-way streets. See if you can guide him home in time to watch his favorite TV show!

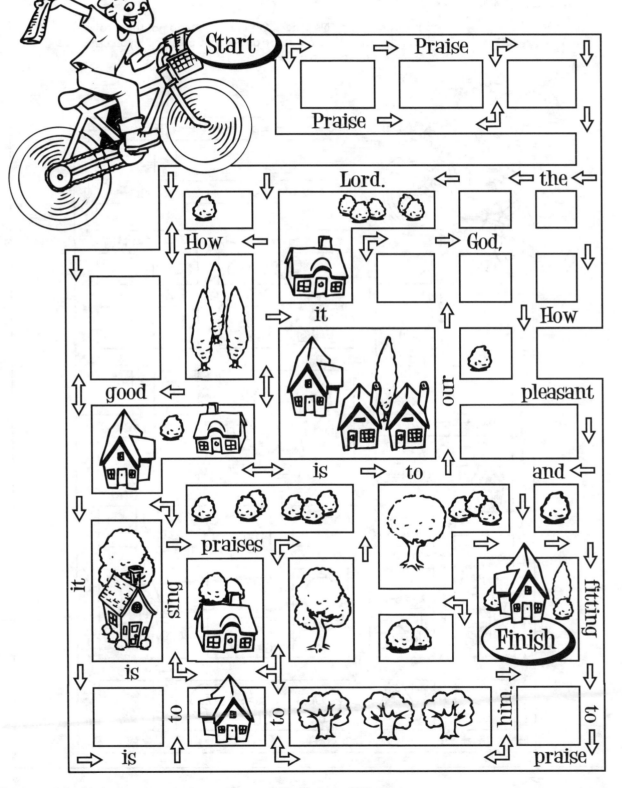

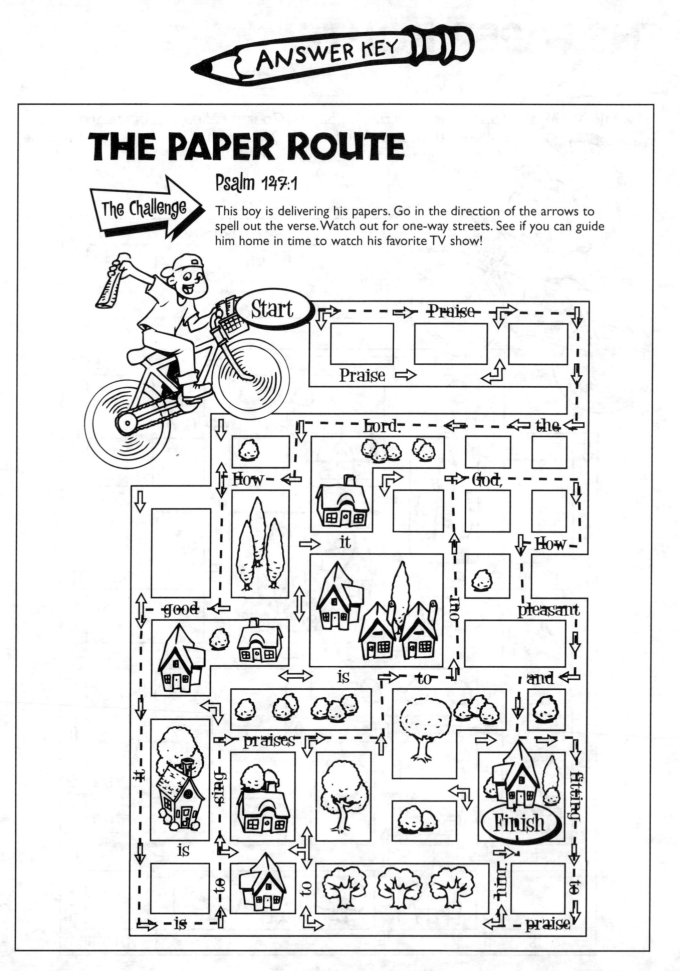

THE PAPER ROUTE

Psalm 147:1

The Challenge

This boy is delivering his papers. Go in the direction of the arrows to spell out the verse. Watch out for one-way streets. See if you can guide him home in time to watch his favorite TV show!

SLIPPED DISCS!

The Challenge

Psalm 149:1

This girl thought she'd slipped a disk when singing along to her pretty funky CD collection. She found a message from the Bible. First she wrote numbers in the squares to put the titles in alphabetical order. Second, she circled the middle word in each CD. Third, she wrote the circled words in order and discovered Psalm 149:1. Can you?

Wally Winkle the Singing Walrus
HOP THE KANGAROO
Vultures of Venus
Rolling Over in the Mud
Four Frogs Sing Ribbett Songs
All Insects Praise the Crickets
Sam and the Snivelling Snake
Lizzie's New Limousine
Newton and His Freaky Frog
Burst All the Party Balloons!

GORILLA KISSES TO YOU ALL!
Peter Pig's Praise of Possums
MY SILLY SONG ABOUT YOU
The School Assembly Album...LiVe
Kiss a Koala!

" _____ _____ Lord. _____

_____ _____ Lord _____

_____ _____ , _____ _____

_____ _____ _____

_____ saints ."

SLIPPED DISCS!

The Challenge →

Psalm 149:1

This girl thought she'd slipped a disk when singing along to her pretty funky CD collection. She found a message from the Bible. First she wrote numbers in the squares to put the titles in alphabetical order. Second, she circled the middle word in each CD. Third, she wrote the circled words in order and discovered Psalm 149:1. Can you?

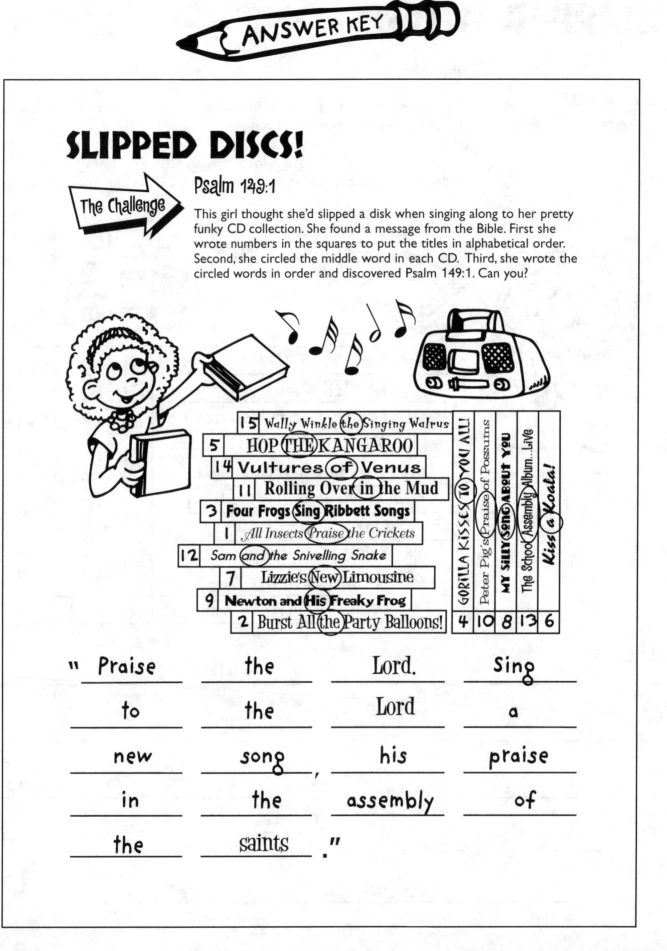

" Praise   the   Lord.   Sing

to   the   Lord   a

new   song ,   his   praise

in   the   assembly   of

the   saints   ."

GO FLY A KITE!

Proverbs 2:6

Follow Ann's kite string to the end, picking up the words you pass as you go. Write down each word in order. Then follow Sam's string and finally Hadiki's string, doing the same. You will find an awesome verse!

"
_____

_____ "

_____ .

GO FLY A KITE!

Proverbs 2:6

The Challenge Follow Ann's kite string to the end, picking up the words you pass as you go. Write down each word in order. Then follow Sam's string and finally Hadiki's string, doing the same. You will find an awesome verse!

" **The Lord gives wisdom, and from his mouth come knowledge and understanding** ."

COMPUTER VIRUS!

Proverbs 3:5,6

The Challenge — The computer has some sort of a glitch. When the verse was input, the words ran together in places and became difficult to read. Can you separate the words and write out the verse correctly?

"Trus tint he Lordwithal lyour
_____

hea rtand leanno ton youro wn
_____

understa nding, inallyour
_____

waysack nowle dgehi mand
_____

hewi llma keyou r
_____

pat hsstr aight."
_____

COMPUTER VIRUS!

Proverbs 3:5,6

The Challenge ➡ The computer has some sort of a glitch. When the verse was input, the words ran together in places and became difficult to read. Can you separate the words and write out the verse correctly?

"Trus tint he Lordwithal lyour

"Trust in the Lord with all your

hea rtand leanno ton youro wn

heart and lean not on your own

understa nding, inallyour

understanding; in all your

waysack nowle dgehi m,and

ways acknowledge him, and

hewi llma keyou r

he will make your

pat hsstr aight."

paths straight."

SPECIAL DELIVERY!

Isaiah 9:6

The Challenge First number all the cribs in alphabetical order. Then write the word or words from each crib on the blank lines below in order to find a verse declaring the birth of Jesus.

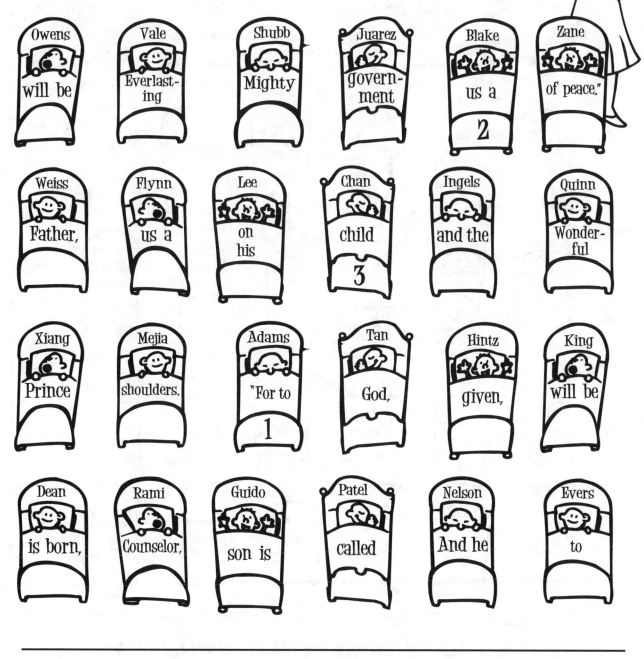

Owens — will be

Vale — Everlast-ing

Shubb — Mighty

Juarez — govern-ment

Blake — us a — 2

Zane — of peace."

Weiss — Father,

Flynn — us a

Lee — on his

Chan — child — 3

Ingels — and the

Quinn — Wonder-ful

Xiang — Prince

Mejia — shoulders.

Adams — "For to — 1

Tan — God,

Hintz — given,

King — will be

Dean — is born,

Rami — Counselor,

Guido — son is

Patel — called

Nelson — And he

Evers — to

_____

_____

_____

_____

SPECIAL DELIVERY!

Isaiah 9:6

The Challenge → First number all the cribs in alphabetical order. Then write the word or words from each crib on the blank lines below in order to find a verse declaring the birth of Jesus.

Owens	Vale	Shubb	Juarez	Blake	Zane
will be	Everlast-ing	Mighty	govern-ment	us a	of peace."
15	21	19	10	2	24

Weiss	Flynn	Lee	Chan	Ingels	Quinn
Father,	us a	on his	child	and the	Wonder-ful
22	6	12	3	9	17

Xiang	Mejia	Adams	Tan	Hintz	King
Prince	shoulders.	"For to	God,	given,	will be
23	13	1	20	8	11

Dean	Rami	Guido	Patel	Nelson	Evers
is born,	Counselor,	son is	called	And he	to
4	18	7	16	14	5

"For to us a child is born, to us a son is given, and the government will be on his shoulders. And he will be called Wonderful Counselor, Mighty God, Everlasting Father, Prince of Peace."

BLANKITY BLANKS

The Challenge

Jeremiah 17:7

This is a real code-breaker puzzle. Each letter of the alphabet has been given a number, but only a few of the letters have been given to you. Write the letters you have been given in the alphabet key. Then see if you can figure out the code and write in the rest of the letters. Use the key to discover the words of the verse.

Alphabet Key:

												28					
A	B	C	D	E	F	G	H	I	J	K	L	M	N	O	P	Q	R	S

T	U	V	W	X	Y	Z

"B __ E __ __ __ __
 4 24 10 38 38 10 8

__ __   __ __ __
18 38   40 16 10

__ __ __ __ __
46 16 30 38 10
__ __ __ __ __
 6 30 28 12 18 -
__ __ __ __ __
 8 10 28 6 10

__ A __
26 2 28
__ __ __
46 16 30
__ __ __ __ __ __
40 36 42 38 40 38

__ __   __ __ __
18 28   40 16 10
__ __ __ __ ,
24 30 36 8

__ __   __ __
18 38   18 28
          "
__ __ __ .
16 18 26

BLANKITY BLANKS

The Challenge

Jeremiah 17:7

This is a real code-breaker puzzle. Each letter of the alphabet has been given a number, but only a few of the letters have been given to you. Write the letters you have been given in the alphabet key. Then see if you can figure out the code and write in the rest of the letters. Use the key to discover the words of the verse.

Alphabet Key:

2	4	6	8	10	12	14	16	18	20	22	24	26	28	30	32	34	36	38
A	B	C	D	E	F	G	H	I	J	K	L	M	N	O	P	Q	R	S

40	42	44	46	48	50	52
T	U	W	W	X	Y	Z

"BLESSED
4 24 10 38 38 10 8

IS   THE
18 38   40 16 10

WHOSE
46 16 30 38 10

CONFI-
6 30 28 12 18

DENCE
8 10 28 6 10

MAN
26 2 28

WHO
46 16 30

TRUSTS
40 36 42 38 40 38

IN   THE
18 28 40 16 10

LORD,
24 30 36 8

IS   IN
18 38 18 28

HIM."
16 18 26

TREASURE TROVE

The Challenge

Daniel 2:20

Ahoy there, mateys! Solve this puzzle and our pirate friend won't make you walk the plank. Use the letter and number under each line to find the coordinate on the map. When you've found each coordinate, unscramble the letters in the square to make a word. Do all 16 to uncover one of God's treasures just for you!

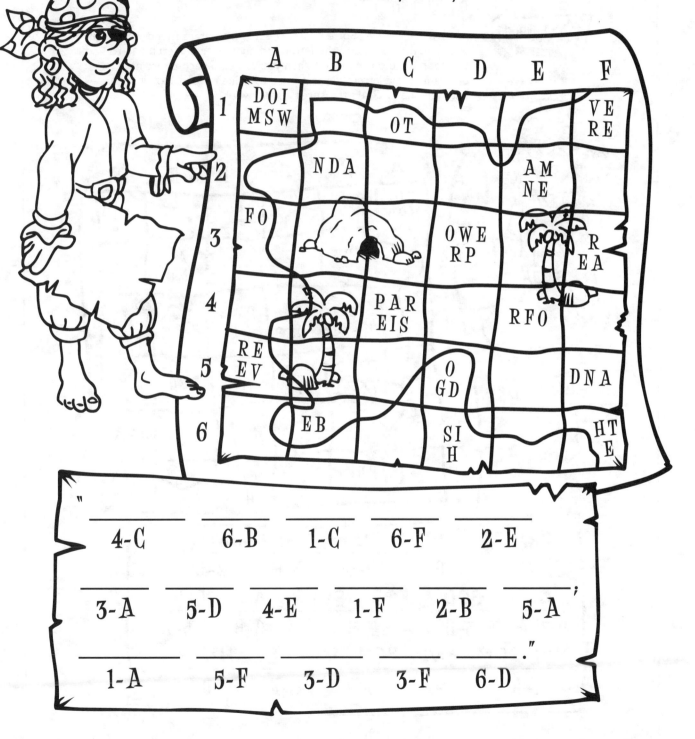

"
___ ___ ___ ___ ___
4-C 6-B 1-C 6-F 2-E

___ ___ ___ ___ ___ ___;
3-A 5-D 4-E 1-F 2-B 5-A

___ ___ ___ ___ ___."
1-A 5-F 3-D 3-F 6-D

TREASURE TROVE

Daniel 2:20

The Challenge → Ahoy there, mateys! Solve this puzzle and our pirate friend won't make you walk the plank. Use the letter and number under each line to find the coordinate on the map. When you've found each coordinate, unscramble the letters in the square to make a word. Do all 16 to uncover one of God's treasures just for you!

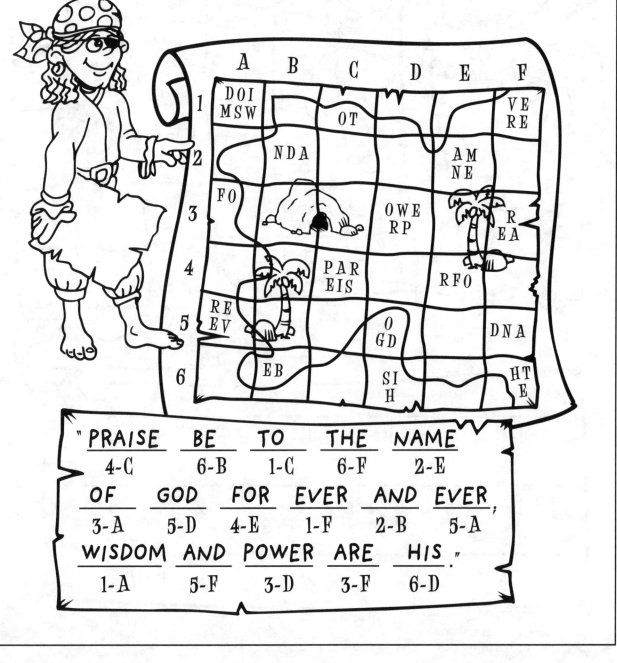

"PRAISE   BE   TO   THE   NAME
4-C   6-B   1-C   6-F   2-E

OF   GOD   FOR   EVER   AND   EVER,
3-A   5-D   4-E   1-F   2-B   5-A

WISDOM   AND   POWER   ARE   HIS."
1-A   5-F   3-D   3-F   6-D

HE'S GOT THE WHOLE WORLD IN HIS HANDS

The Challenge

Zechariah 14:9

Travel around the world to solve this puzzle. Start at the center star each time you need a letter. Some letters will be repeated.

The first clue is NW-1. NW-1 means you go northwest from the star one letter. So the first letter you find is the letter *T*, which you write on blank 1. It's also used on blank 22. Now do the rest.

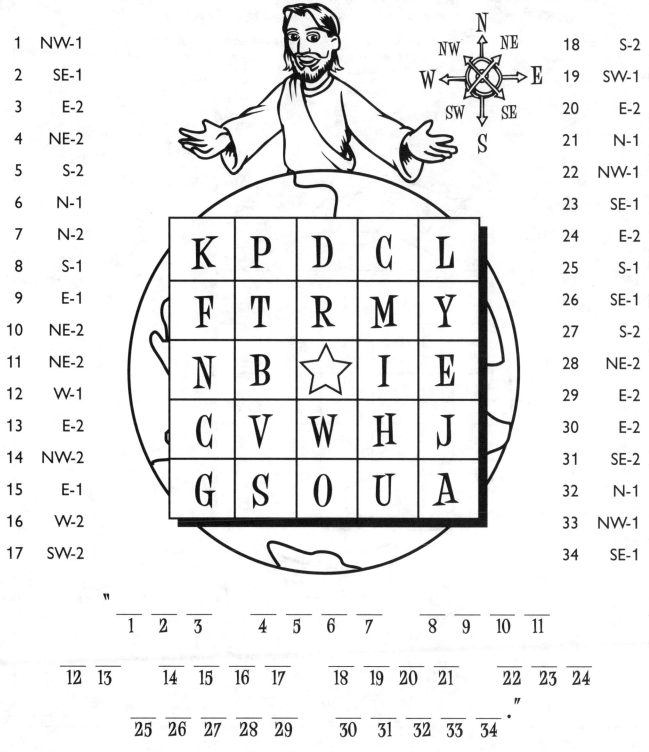

1　NW-1
2　SE-1
3　E-2
4　NE-2
5　S-2
6　N-1
7　N-2
8　S-1
9　E-1
10　NE-2
11　NE-2
12　W-1
13　E-2
14　NW-2
15　E-1
16　W-2
17　SW-2

18　S-2
19　SW-1
20　E-2
21　N-1
22　NW-1
23　SE-1
24　E-2
25　S-1
26　SE-1
27　S-2
28　NE-2
29　E-2
30　E-2
31　SE-2
32　N-1
33　NW-1
34　SE-1

" __ __ __ __ __ __ __ __ __ __ __
　1　2　3　　4　5　6　7　　8　9　10　11

__ __ __ __ __ __ __ __ __ __ __ __ __
12　13　14　15　16　17　18　19　20　21　22　23　24

__ __ __ __ __ __ __ __ __ __ ."
25　26　27　28　29　30　31　32　33　34

HE'S GOT THE WHOLE WORLD IN HIS HANDS

Zechariah 14:9

Travel around the world to solve this puzzle. Start at the center star each time you need a letter. Some letters will be repeated.

The first clue is NW-1. NW-1 means you go northwest from the star one letter. So the first letter you find is the letter *T*, which you write on blank 1. It's also used on blank 22. Now do the rest.

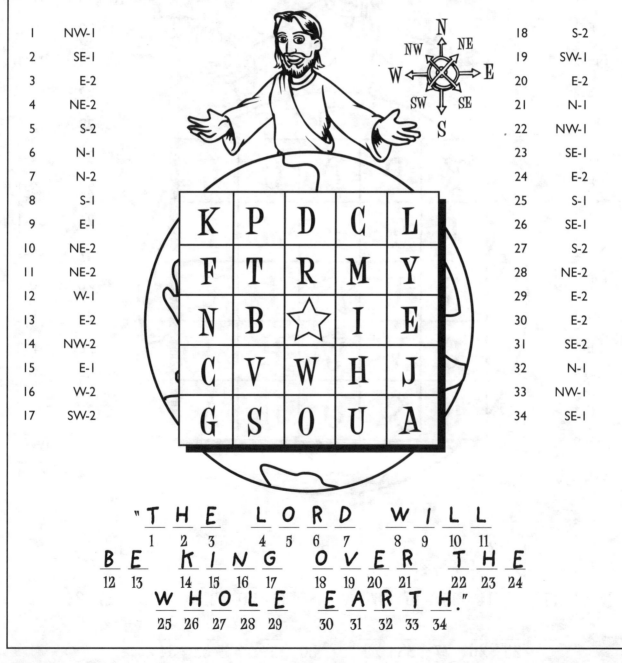

1	NW-1
2	SE-1
3	E-2
4	NE-2
5	S-2
6	N-1
7	N-2
8	S-1
9	E-1
10	NE-2
11	NE-2
12	W-1
13	E-2
14	NW-2
15	E-1
16	W-2
17	SW-2

18	S-2
19	SW-1
20	E-2
21	N-1
22	NW-1
23	SE-1
24	E-2
25	S-1
26	SE-1
27	S-2
28	NE-2
29	E-2
30	E-2
31	SE-2
32	N-1
33	NW-1
34	SE-1

Grid:

K	P	D	C	L
F	T	R	M	Y
N	B	☆	I	E
C	V	W	H	J
G	S	O	U	A

"THE LORD WILL
1 2 3   4 5 6 7   8 9 10 11

BE KING OVER THE
12 13   14 15 16 17   18 19 20 21   22 23 24

WHOLE EARTH."
25 26 27 28 29   30 31 32 33 34

THREE-RING CIRCUS!

Mark 12:30

"Love the Lord your God with all your heart and with all your soul and with all your mind and with all your strength."

The Challenge ▶ As you go through the maze, pass the four things with which you can love God in the order they are in the verse. You cannot cross or retrace your path. Finish where you started.

THREE-RING CIRCUS!

Mark 12:30

"Love the Lord your God with all your heart and with all your soul and with all your mind and with all your strength."

The Challenge → As you go through the maze, pass the four things with which you can love God in the order they are in the verse. You cannot cross or retrace your path. Finish where you started.

THE JIG IS UP!

Luke 1:46,47

Match the shapes to find the letters that belong in each jigsaw shape. Write in the words to read the verse.

THE JIG IS UP!

Luke 1:46,47

The Challenge → Match the shapes to find the letters that belong in each jigsaw shape. Write in the words to read the verse.

VIDEO VERSE

Luke 6:27

These kids are trying to discover the hidden message on the wall. Fill in the clues. Decipher the message by writing on the blank lines only the letters in the squares.

The opposite of hate
☐ ☐ ☐ ☐

A popular toy
Y O - ☐ ☐

Animal covering
F ☐ ☐

The number after nine
T ☐ ☐

Another name for a jewel
G ☐ ☐

Tells a fib
L ☐ ☐ ☐

Not a cat but a
☐ ☐ G

The opposite of bad
☐ ☐ ☐ ☐

The number after one
☐ W ☐

The planet we live on
E A R ☐ ☐

A fragrant flower
R ☐ ☐ ☐

Two halves equal a
☐ ☐ ☐ L E

The opposite of love
☐ ☐ ☐

Not me but
☐ ☐ ☐

_____

_____

_____

VIDEO VERSE

Luke 6:27

The Challenge ➤ These kids are trying to discover the hidden message on the wall. Fill in the clues. Decipher the message by writing on the blank lines only the letters in the squares.

The opposite of hate	A popular toy	Animal covering	The number after nine
L [O] V E	Y O - [YO]	F [UR] R	T [EN] N
Another name for a jewel	Tells a fib	Not a cat but a	The opposite of bad
G [EM] M	L [IES] S	[DO] G	[GOOD]
The number after one	The planet we live on	A fragrant flower	Two halves equal a
[T] W [O]	E A R [TH]	R [OSE] E	[WHO] L E
The opposite of love	Not me but		
[HATE]	[YOU]		

LOVE YOUR ENEMIES

DO GOOD TO THOSE WHO HATE YOU

HEART TO HEART!

Luke 6:37

Drop the letters one by one into the boxes below to discover this verse from God's heart to yours! Cross off letters as you use them. The first word has been done for you.

(HINT: Look up Luke 6:37 to help solve the puzzle!)

HEART TO HEART!

Luke 6:37

The Challenge → Drop the letters one by one into the boxes below to discover this verse from God's heart to yours! Cross off letters as you use them. The first word has been done for you.

Y O R O W V L L A B E
F O U G X I N N D
X O K I X E

F	O	R	G	I	V	E			A	N	D
Y	O	U		W	I	L	L			B	E
F	O	R	G	I	V	E	N		

(HINT: Look up Luke 6:37 to help solve the puzzle!)

DIZZY SPELLS!

John 3:16

These kids are getting dizzy trying to solve this puzzle! Start at the center of the spiral and fill in the missing vowels. After you do, memorize the verse. (Hint: Read the verse in your Bible for help.)

DIZZY SPELLS!

John 3:16

The Challenge → These kids are getting dizzy trying to solve this puzzle! Start at the center of the spiral and fill in the missing vowels. After you do, memorize the verse. (Hint: Read the verse in your Bible for help.)

LIGHTEN UP!

John 8:12

The Challenge

Everybody loves word search puzzles! Here's one about all sorts of lights. To find these sources of light, look up, down, backwards and diagonally.

campfire
candle
firefly
fireworks
flashlight
headlight
lamp
lantern
lightbulb
lighthouse
lightning
match
spark
star
sun
torch

```
L  A  N  T  E  R  N  T  H  E  L
C  I  E  K  R  A  P  S  F  S  I
T  A  G  L  I  G  H  N  I  U  G
H  H  M  H  T  C  U  C  R  O  H
G  S  O  P  T  S  F  A  E  H  T
I  T  T  A  F  B  H  N  F  T  N
L  P  M  A  L  I  U  D  L  H  I
D  E  W  O  R  R  R  L  Y  G  N
A  L  H  C  R  O  T  E  B  I  G
E  T  H  G  I  L  H  S  A  L  F
H  F  I  R  E  W  O  R  K  S  D
```

The Super Challenge

Find the letters that you didn't circle from left to right, top to bottom, and write them on the blanks in order. You'll find out something special about Jesus.

"[Jesus] said, 'I am __ __ __ __ __   __ __ __ __ __

__ __ __ __ __ __   __ __ __ __ __ __ __.'"

LIGHTEN UP!

John 8:12

The Challenge

Everybody loves word search puzzles! Here's one about all sorts of lights. To find these sources of light, look up, down, backwards and diagonally.

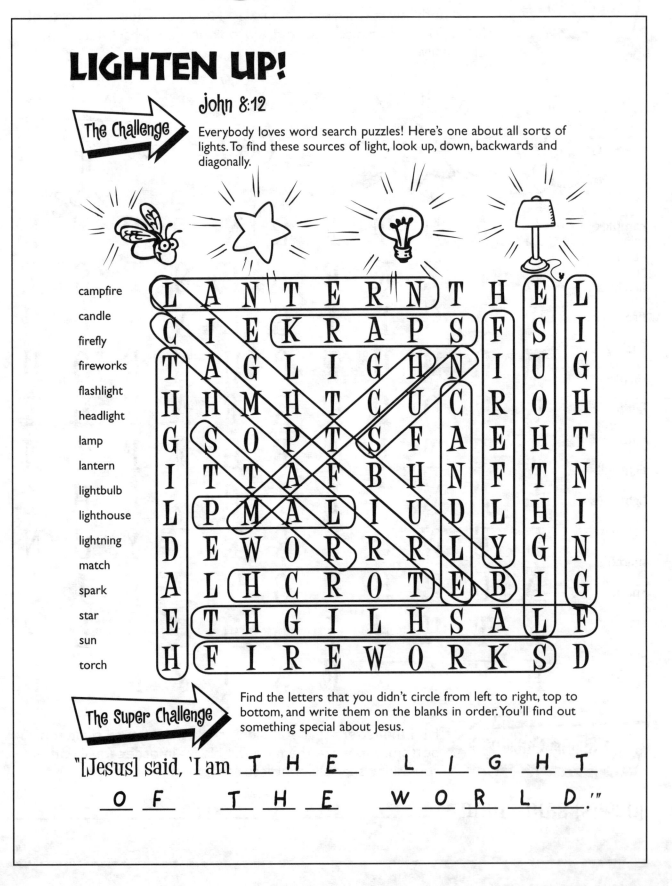

campfire
candle
firefly
fireworks
flashlight
headlight
lamp
lantern
lightbulb
lighthouse
lightning
match
spark
star
sun
torch

The Super Challenge

Find the letters that you didn't circle from left to right, top to bottom, and write them on the blanks in order. You'll find out something special about Jesus.

"[Jesus] said, 'I am **T H E   L I G H T   O F   T H E   W O R L D**.'"

BINGO!

The Challenge

John 14:3

Fill in the blanks below by finding each word that matches the bingo letters. Then you can read the verse.

B	I	N	G	O
6 you	16 with	25 will	4 go	28 for
18 you	5 place	13 If	7 am	11 may
12 back	The God's Special Promise Bingo Game			24 that
20 you	8 take	19 I	2 and	27 where
3 I	17 I	21 me	14 to	9 a
10 be	23 prepare	1 also	26 come	15 and

"

| N-13 | N-19 | G-4 | O-15 | I-23 | O-9 | I-5 |

| O-28 | B-6 ' | I-17 | N-25 | G-26 | B-12 | G-2 |

| I-8 | B-18 | G-14 | B-10 | I-16 | N-21 | O-24 " |

| B-20 | N-1 | O-11 | B-10 | O-27 | B-3 | G-7 . |

BINGO!

The Challenge

John 14:3

Fill in the blanks below by finding each word that matches the bingo letters. Then you can read the verse.

B	I	N	G	O
6 you	16 with	25 will	4 go	28 for
18 you	5 place	13 If	7 am	11 may
12 back	The God's Special	Promise Bingo Game		24 that
20 you	8 take	19 I	2 and	27 where
3 I	17 I	21 me	14 to	9 a
10 be	23 prepare	1 also	26 come	15 and

" If   I   go   and   prepare   a   place
N-13   N-19   G-4   O-15   I-23   O-9   I-5

for   you   I   will   come   back   and
O-28   B-6 ,   I-17   N-25   G-26   B-12   G-2

take   you   to   be   with   me   that
I-8   B-18   G-14   B-10   I-16   N-21   O-24 "

you   also   may   be   where   I   am
B-20   N-1   O-11   B-10   O-27   B-3   G-7 .

PICTURE THIS!

The Challenge

John 14:27

Unscramble the words on the easel to decipher the verse.

"_____ _____ _____
E A E C P   I   V E E A L

_____ _____; _____ _____
T H I W   U Y O   Y M

_____ _____ _____
E A E C P   I   V I G E

_____ .... _____ _____ _____
O U Y   O D   O N T   E T L

_____ _____ _____
R O Y U   E R A H T S   E B

_____
B R O T U E D L

_____ _____ _____
D A N   O D   O N T

_____ _____"
E B   F A R I D A

PICTURE THIS!

John 14:27

The Challenge → Unscramble the words on the easel to decipher the verse.

" PEACE   I   LEAVE
  EAECP   I   VEEAL
WITH   YOU ; MY
 THIW   UYO   YM
PEACE   I   GIVE
 EAECP   I   VIGE
YOU ..... DO   NOT   LET
 OUY   OD   ONT   ETL
YOUR   HEART   BE
 ROYU   ERAHTS   EB
  TROUBLED
  BROTUEDL
AND   DO   NOT
 DAN   OD   ONT
BE   AFRAID   ."
 EB   FARIDA

IN STEP WITH JESUS

Acts 10:43

"Everyone who believes in him receives forgiveness of sins through his name."

The Challenge →

Start at the stone the boy is standing on and trace each letter of the verse until you reach Jesus at the end of the maze.

IN STEP WITH JESUS

Acts 10:43

"Everyone who believes in him receives forgiveness of sins through his name."

The Challenge ➡️ Start at the stone the boy is standing on and trace each letter of the verse until you reach Jesus at the end of the maze.

THE TALK OF THE TOWN!

Acts 28:31

The Challenge →

"Boldly and without hindrance he preached the kingdom of God and taught about the Lord Jesus Christ."

All the words from the verse can be filled in the crossword grid. Are you up to the challenge?

2 Letters
he
of

3 Letters
and
and
God
the
the

4 Letters
Lord

5 Letters
about
Jesus

6 Letters
Boldly
Christ
taught

7 Letters
kingdom
without

8 Letters
preached

9 Letters
hindrance

THE TALK OF THE TOWN!

The Challenge

Acts 28:31

"Boldly and without hindrance he preached the kingdom of God and taught about the Lord Jesus Christ."

All the words from the verse can be filled in the crossword grid. Are you up to the challenge?

2 Letters
he
of

3 Letters
and
and
God
the
the

4 Letters
Lord

5 Letters
about
~~Jesus~~

6 Letters
Boldly
Christ
taught

7 Letters
kingdom
without

8 Letters
preached

9 Letters
hindrance

IT'S A DOG'S LIFE!

Romans 8:28

The Challenge → Uh-oh. The dog has torn up the Bible verse. Can you put the pieces together and then memorize the verse?

things know to his of

have

"We who according

that

works for the good

been those who

called

purpose."

love him,

in all

God

IT'S A DOG'S LIFE!

Romans 8:28

The Challenge

Uh-oh. The dog has torn up the Bible verse. Can you put the pieces together and then memorize the verse?

"We know that in all things God works for the good of those who love him, who have been called according to his purpose."

THE WRITING'S ON THE WALL!

1 Corinthians 12:27

The Challenge → These kids have built a big wall that's hiding the Bible verse. Follow the instructions to read the verse. Write the leftover words in order on the blank lines.

Step 1: Cross out all the names of colors.

Step 2: Cross out all the types of transportation.

Step 3: Lose the girls' names.

Step 4: Hey, why pick on the girls? Cross out the boys' names, too.

Step 5: Who needs the names of different toys? You don't.

Step 6. Finally, let's get rid of the school subjects. (Hey, it's only for this puzzle!)

blue	bicycle	Now	Scott	you
ball	are	science	airplane	Zack
Amy	kite	turquoise	the	yo-yo
mathematics	body	motorcycle	Joshua	
of	reading	Emily	Christ,	puzzle
boat	spelling	and	magenta	Dylan
car	Jessica	balloon	each	one
of	history	you	skateboard	Tyler
Bartholomew	is	a	truck	part
of	Michelle	lavender	jump rope	it

"

_____

_____ ."

THE WRITING'S ON THE WALL!

1 Corinthians 12:27

The Challenge These kids have built a big wall that's hiding the Bible verse. Follow the instructions to read the verse. Write the leftover words in order on the blank lines.

Step 1: Cross out all the names of colors.

Step 2: Cross out all the types of transportation.

Step 3: Lose the girls' names.

Step 4: Hey, why pick on the girls? Cross out the boys' names, too.

Step 5: Who needs the names of different toys? You don't.

Step 6. Finally, let's get rid of the school subjects. (Hey, it's only for this puzzle!)

" <u>Now you are the body of Christ,</u>

<u>and each one of you is a part of it</u>   "

PICTURE PERFECT!

1 Corinthians 13:4

The Challenge ➡

Write the first letter of each picture in the grid below. Then write those letters in the matching blanks. You will find the words of the verse.

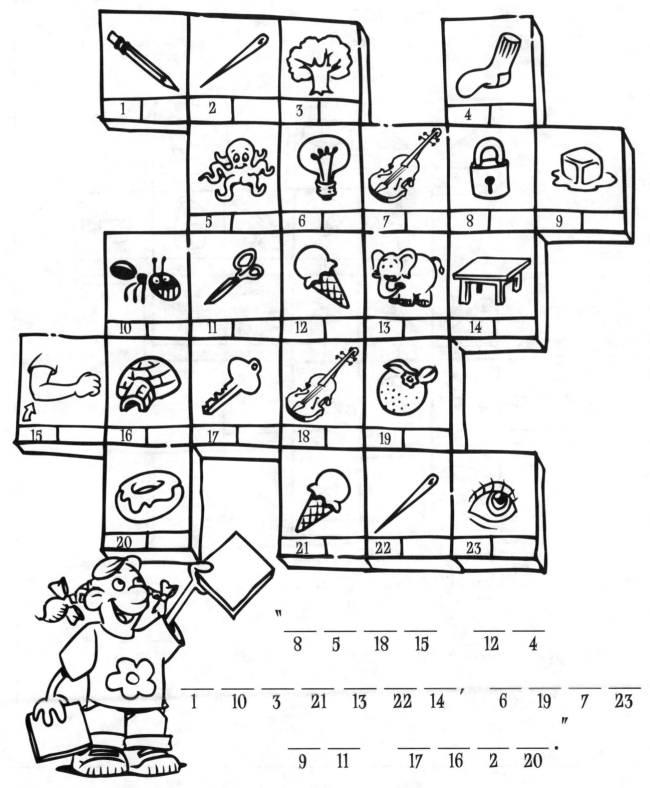

"
$\overline{}_{8}$ $\overline{}_{5}$ $\overline{}_{18}$ $\overline{}_{15}$ $\overline{}_{12}$ $\overline{}_{4}$

$\overline{}_{1}$ $\overline{}_{10}$ $\overline{}_{3}$ $\overline{}_{21}$ $\overline{}_{13}$ $\overline{}_{22}$ $\overline{}_{14}$, $\overline{}_{6}$ $\overline{}_{19}$ $\overline{}_{7}$ $\overline{}_{23}$ "

$\overline{}_{9}$ $\overline{}_{11}$ $\overline{}_{17}$ $\overline{}_{16}$ $\overline{}_{2}$ $\overline{}_{20}$.

PICTURE PERFECT!

1 Corinthians 13:4

The Challenge → Write the first letter of each picture in the grid below. Then write those letters in the matching blanks. You will find the words of the verse.

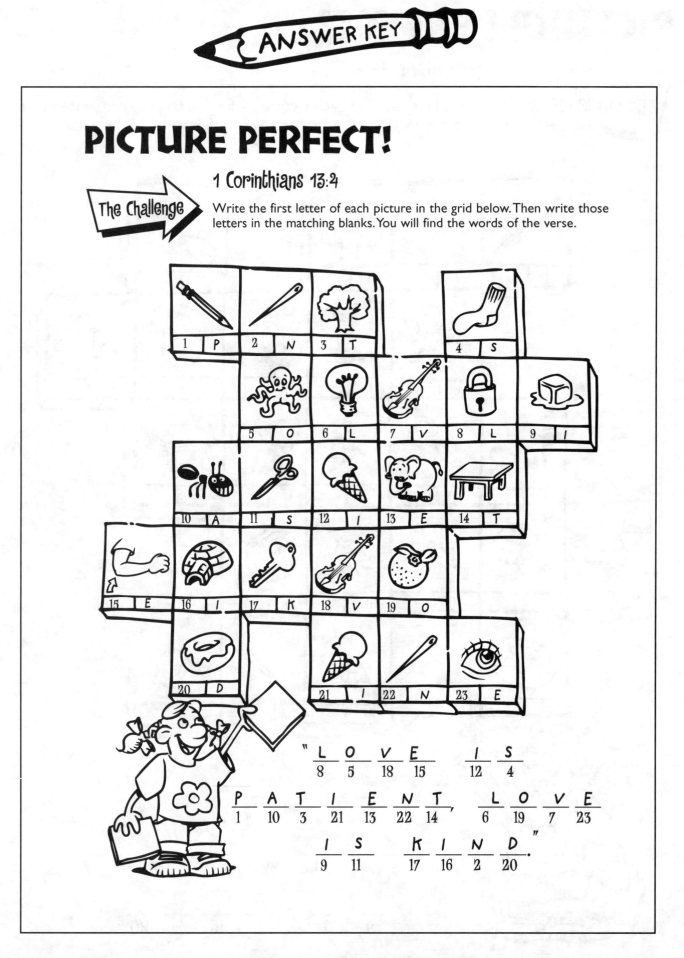

1 P	2 N	3 T		4 S
5 O	6 L	7 V	8 L	9 I
10 A	11 S	12 I	13 E	14 T
15 E	16 I	17 K	18 V	19 O
20 D		21 I	22 N	23 E

" L O V E   I S
  8 5 18 15 12 4

P A T I E N T,   L O V E
1 10 3 21 13 22 14   6 19 7 23

I S   K I N D."
9 11   17 16 2 20

GIMME A HIGH FIVE!

1 Corinthians 13:7

The Challenge Solve the code below to write out a special verse about love.

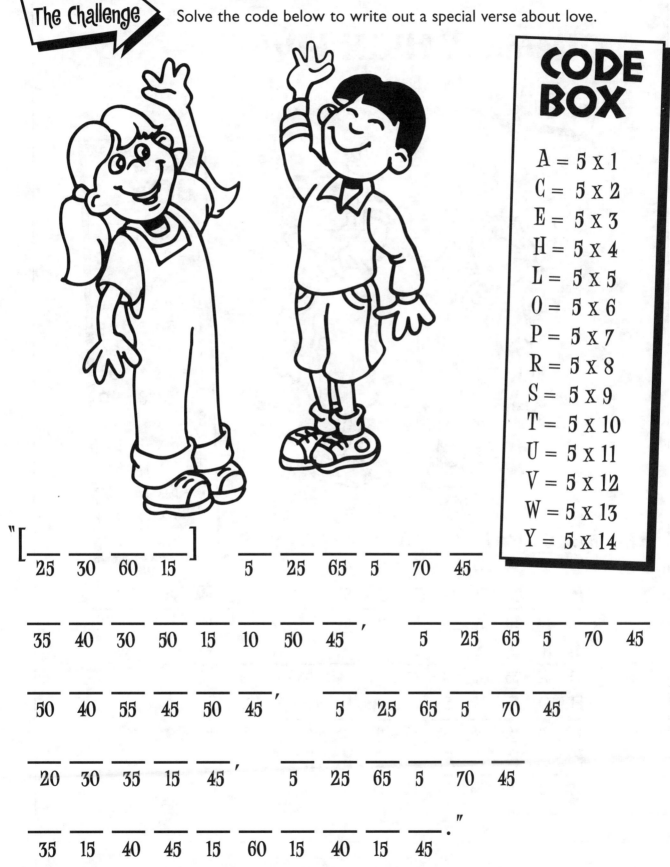

CODE BOX

A = 5 x 1
C = 5 x 2
E = 5 x 3
H = 5 x 4
L = 5 x 5
O = 5 x 6
P = 5 x 7
R = 5 x 8
S = 5 x 9
T = 5 x 10
U = 5 x 11
V = 5 x 12
W = 5 x 13
Y = 5 x 14

" [__ __ __ __]   __ __ __ __ __ __
   25 30 60 15   5 25 65 5 70 45

__ __ __ __ __ __ __ __ ,   __ __ __ __ __ __
35 40 30 50 15 10 50 45   5 25 65 5 70 45

__ __ __ __ __ __ ,   __ __ __ __ __ __
50 40 55 45 50 45   5 25 65 5 70 45

__ __ __ __ __ ,   __ __ __ __ __ __
20 30 35 15 45   5 25 65 5 70 45

__ __ __ __ __ __ __ __ __ __ . "
35 15 40 45 15 60 15 40 15 45

GIMME A HIGH FIVE!

1 Corinthians 13:7

The Challenge ➡ Solve the code below to write out a special verse about love.

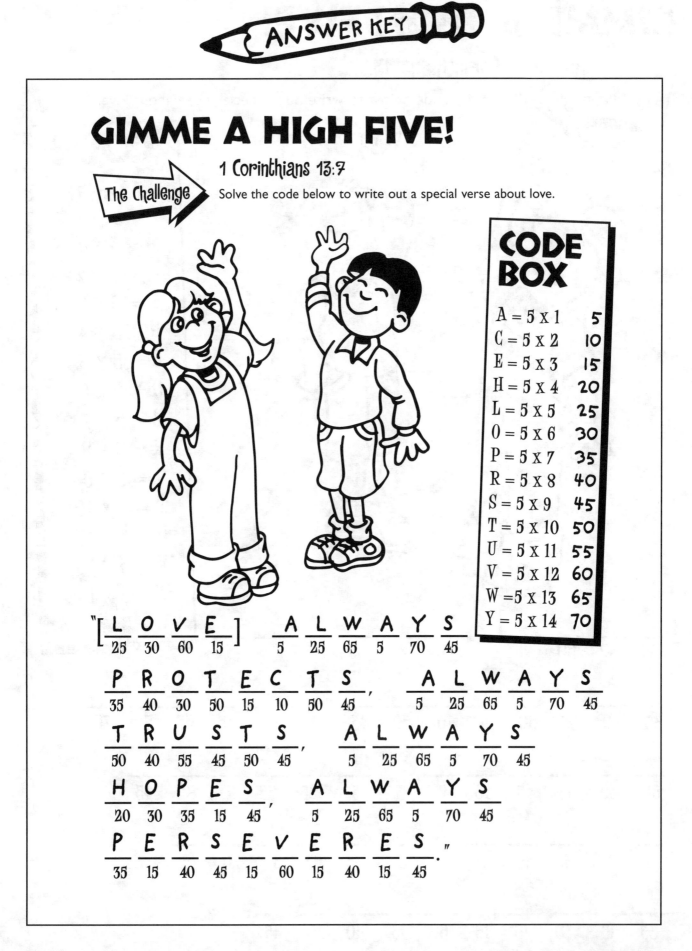

CODE BOX

A = 5 x 1	5
C = 5 x 2	10
E = 5 x 3	15
H = 5 x 4	20
L = 5 x 5	25
O = 5 x 6	30
P = 5 x 7	35
R = 5 x 8	40
S = 5 x 9	45
T = 5 x 10	50
U = 5 x 11	55
V = 5 x 12	60
W = 5 x 13	65
Y = 5 x 14	70

"[L O V E]   A L W A Y S
  25 30 60 15   5 25 65 5 70 45

P R O T E C T S ,   A L W A Y S
35 40 30 50 15 10 50 45   5 25 65 5 70 45

T R U S T S ,   A L W A Y S
50 40 55 45 50 45   5 25 65 5 70 45

H O P E S ,   A L W A Y S
20 30 35 15 45   5 25 65 5 70 45

P E R S E V E R E S . "
35 15 40 45 15 60 15 40 15 45

BUTTERFLY KISSES!

2 Corinthians 5:17

 **The Challenge** As you know, some caterpillars change into butterflies, just as if they were new creations. The caterpillars below are changing into butterflies. Find the hidden number on each butterfly and caterpillar and then write the words of the verse in order. Just for fun, circle the one caterpillar who hasn't changed into a matching butterfly!

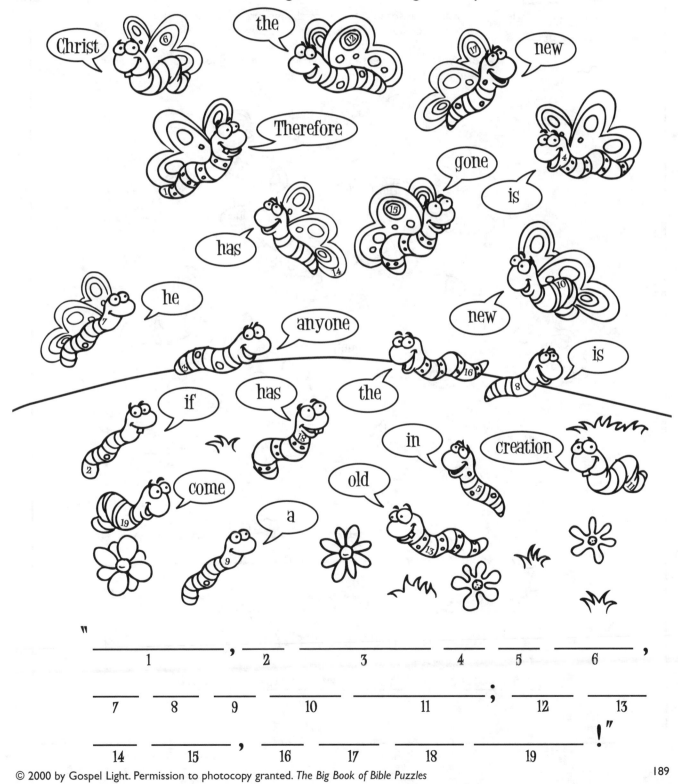

"_____ , _____ _____ _____ _____ _____ ,
    1   2   3   4   5   6

_____ _____ _____ _____ _____ ; _____ _____
  7   8   9   10   11   12   13

_____ _____ , _____ _____ _____ _____ !"
  14   15   16   17   18   19

BUTTERFLY KISSES!

2 Corinthians 5:17

The Challenge →

As you know, some caterpillars change into butterflies, just as if they were new creations. The caterpillars below are changing into butterflies. Find the hidden number on each butterfly and caterpillar and then write the words of the verse in order. Just for fun, circle the one caterpillar who hasn't changed into a matching butterfly!

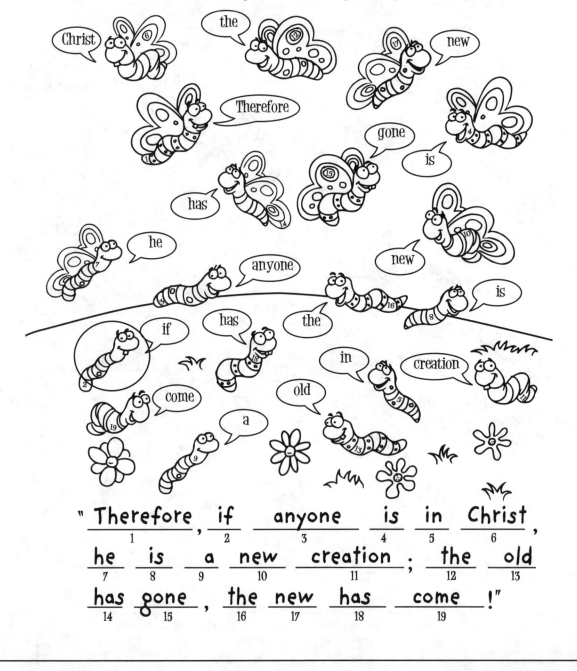

" <u>Therefore</u> , <u>if</u> <u>anyone</u> <u>is</u> <u>in</u> <u>Christ</u> ,
   1   2   3   4   5   6

<u>he</u> <u>is</u> <u>a</u> <u>new</u> <u>creation</u> ; <u>the</u> <u>old</u>
 7   8   9   10   11   12   13

<u>has</u> <u>gone</u> , <u>the</u> <u>new</u> <u>has</u> <u>come</u> !"
 14   15   16   17   18   19

IT'S A WRAP!

Ephesians 2:8,9

"For it is by grace you have been saved, through faith—and this not from yourselves, it is the gift of God—not by works, so that no one can boast."

The Challenge

Hidden in this very unusual wrapping paper are most of the words from Ephesians 2: 8,9. Starting at the square on the top left-hand side, see if you can make it all the way to the girl, who finishes the verses for you.

IT'S A WRAP!

Ephesians 2:8,9

"For it is by grace you have been saved, through faith—and this not from yourselves, it is the gift of God—not by works, so that no one can boast."

 **The Challenge** Hidden in this very unusual wrapping paper are most of the words from Ephesians 2: 8,9. Starting at the square on the top left-hand side, see if you can make it all the way to the girl, who finishes the verses for you.

GOD'S GOT YOUR NUMBER!

Ephesians 4:32

The Challenge → Use the number code below to discover the words of the verse.

A=1   B=2   C=3   D=4   E=5   F=6
G=7   H=8   I=9   J=10   K=11   L=12
M=13   N=14   O=15   P=16   Q=17
R=18   S=19   T=20   U=21   V=22
W=23   X=24   Y=25   Z=26

2.5   /   11.9.14.4   /   1.14.4   /

" ___ ___   ___ ___ ___ ___   ___ ___ ___

3.15.13.16.1.19.19.9.15.14.1.20.5   /

___ ___ ___ ___ ___ ___ ___ ___ ___ ___ ___ ___ ___

20.15   /   15.14.5   /   1 14.15.20.8.5.18   /

___ ___   ___ ___ ___   ___ ___ ___ ___ ___ ___ —,

6.15.18.7.9.22.9.14.7   /

___ ___ ___ ___ ___ ___ ___ ___ ___

5.1.3.8   /   15.20.8.5.18   /

___ ___ ___ ___   ___ ___ ___ ___ ___ —,

10.21.19.20   /   1.19   /   9.14   /

___ ___ ___ ___   ___ ___   ___ ___

3.8.18.9.19.20   /   7.15.4   /

___ ___ ___ ___ ___ ___   ___ ___ ___

6.15.18.7.1.22.5   /   25.15.21   /

___ ___ ___ ___ ___ ___   ___ ___ ___

___ ___ ___ ___ ___ ___ ___ ___ . "

GOD'S GOT YOUR NUMBER!

The Challenge

Ephesians 4:32

Use the number code below to discover the words of the verse.

A=1 B=2 C=3 D=4 E=5 F=6
G=7 H=8 I=9 J=10 K=11 L=12
M=13 N=14 O=15 P=16 Q=17
R=18 S=19 T=20 U=21 V=22
W=23 X=24 Y=25 Z=26

2.5 / 11.9.14.4 / 1.14.4 /
"Be kind and

3.15.13.16.1.19.19.9.15.14.1.20.5 /
compassionate

20.15 / 15.14.5 / 1.14.15.20.8.5.18 /
to one another,

6.15.18.7.9.22.9.14.7 /
forgiving

5.1.3.8 / 15.20.8.5.18 /
each other,

10.21.19.20 / 1.19 / 9.14 /
just as in

3.8.18.9.19.20 / 7.15.4 /
Christ God

6.15.18.7.1.22.5 / 25.15.21 /
forgave you."

ALPHABETICAL ORDER

Philippians 4:6

Work your way through the alphabet magnets. Write the word you read on the letter *A* in the first blank below and then write the word you read on the *B* in the second blank below. Go through the alphabet, filling in the blanks as you go, to find a Bible verse that will help you pray.

" ___ ___ ___ ___ ___ ___ , ___
    A   B   C   D   E   F   G

___ ___ , ___ ___ ___ , ___
    H   I   J   K   L   M   N

___ ___ , ___ ___ ___ ___ . "
    O   P   Q   R   S   T

ALPHABETICAL ORDER

The Challenge

Philippians 4:6

Work your way through the alphabet magnets. Write the word you read on the letter *A* in the first blank below and then write the word you read on the *B* in the second blank below. Go through the alphabet, filling in the blanks as you go, to find a Bible verse that will help you pray.

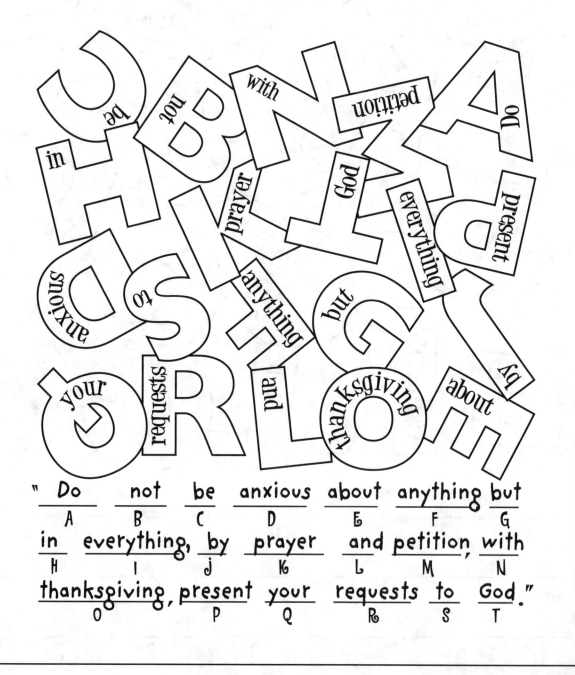

" Do   not   be   anxious   about   anything   but
  A   B   C   D   E   F   G

in   everything,   by   prayer   and   petition,   with
H   I   J   K   L   M   N

thanksgiving,   present   your   requests   to   God."
O   P   Q   R   S   T

GOD FEEDS NEEDS!

Philippians 4:19

 The Challenge

These papers have gotten all mixed up, but if you write the words from each paper in order on the numbered lines below, you will find the Bible verse.

GOD FEEDS NEEDS!

Philippians 4:19

The Challenge → These papers have gotten all mixed up, but if you write the words from each paper in order on the numbered lines below, you will find the Bible verse.

"My God will meet all your needs according to his glorious riches in Christ Jesus."

THE JOKE'S ON YOU!

The Challenge

1 Thessalonians 5:11

Someone's been clowning around and has taken all the letters away from the Bible verse. Fix the verse by following the path from each number to a letter. Then write the letters on the matching blanks.

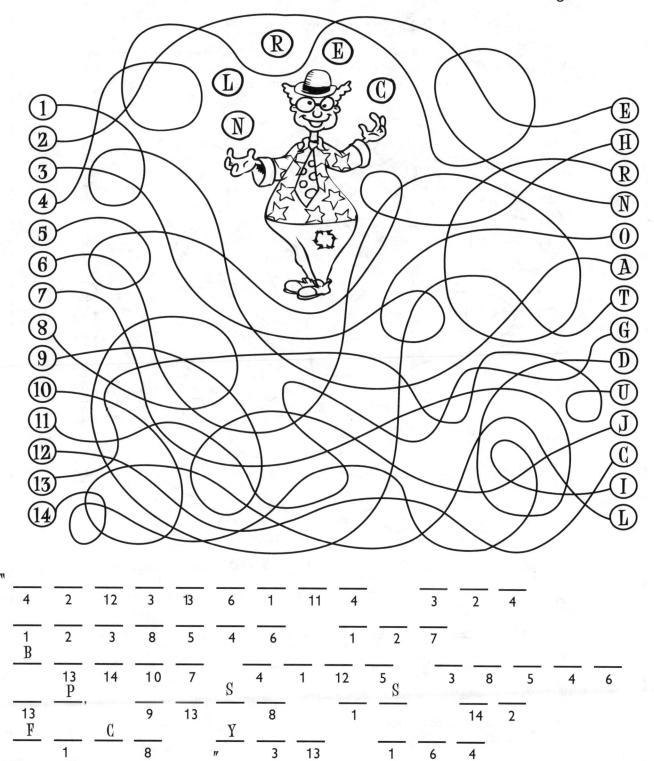

THE JOKE'S ON YOU!

1 Thessalonians 5:11

The Challenge

Someone's been clowning around and has taken all the letters away from the Bible verse. Fix the verse by following the path from each number to a letter. Then write the letters on the matching blanks.

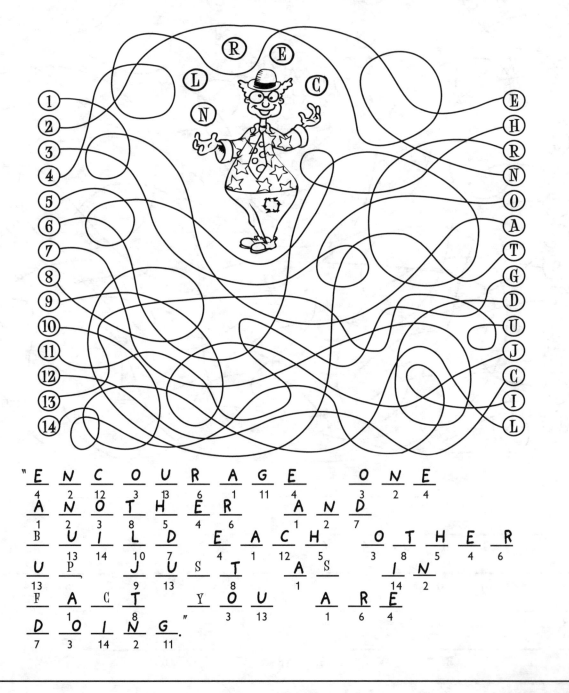

```
" E  N  C  O  U  R  A  G  E     O  N  E
  4  2  12 3  13 6  1  11 4     3  2  4
  A  N  O  T  H  E  R     A  N  D
  1  2  3  8  5  4  6     1  2  7
  B  U  I  L  D     E  A  C  H     O  T  H  E  R
     13 14 10 7     4  1  12 5     3  8  5  4  6
  U  P     J  U  S  T     A  S     I  N
  13    9  13    8     1        14 2
  F  A  C  T     Y  O  U     A  R  E
     1     8     3  13    1  6  4
  D  O  I  N  G  . "
  7  3  14 2  11
```

A SILLY STRING THING!

1 Timothy 2:3, 4

Silly String is fun. Can you reach the TRUTH by starting at the Silly String can? As you go through the maze, pick up the words to spell out the verse. Write the words on the blank lines.

" _____ _____ _____ _____ ...

_____ _____ _____ _____ _____

_____ _____ _____ _____ _____ _____ . "

A SILLY STRING THING!

1 Timothy 2:3, 4

The Challenge → Silly String is fun. Can you reach the TRUTH by starting at the Silly String can? As you go through the maze, pick up the words to spell out the verse. Write the words on the blank lines.

"God our Savior ... wants all men to be saved and to come to a knowledge of the truth."

AT YOUR SERVICE!

1 Peter 4:10

The Challenge

"Each one should use whatever gift he has received to serve others."

Go through the maze, passing the words of the Bible verse in order to find the correct path.

Start

Finish

gift

he

received

gift

others

Each

whatever

whatever

to

serve

should

has

one

should

use

to

use

serve

received

others

use

AT YOUR SERVICE!

1 Peter 4:10

The Challenge

"Each one should use whatever gift he has received to serve others."

Go through the maze, passing the words of the Bible verse in order to find the correct path.

HEADS UP!

1 John 3:1

"How great is the love the Father has lavished on us, that we should be called children of God!"

The Challenge

To go through the maze correctly, find the words of the verse in order. Don't skip over any heads. You will be able to get through it by going directly from head to head.

Start

HEADS UP!

1 John 3:1

The Challenge

"How great is the love the Father has lavished on us, that we should be called children of God!"

To go through the maze correctly, find the words of the verse in order. Don't skip over any heads. You will be able to get through it by going directly from head to head.

HEARTSTRINGS!

1 John 3:16

The Challenge → If you go through the maze correctly by passing through each heart, you'll find the verse. You can't use any heart more than once or cross over your own path.

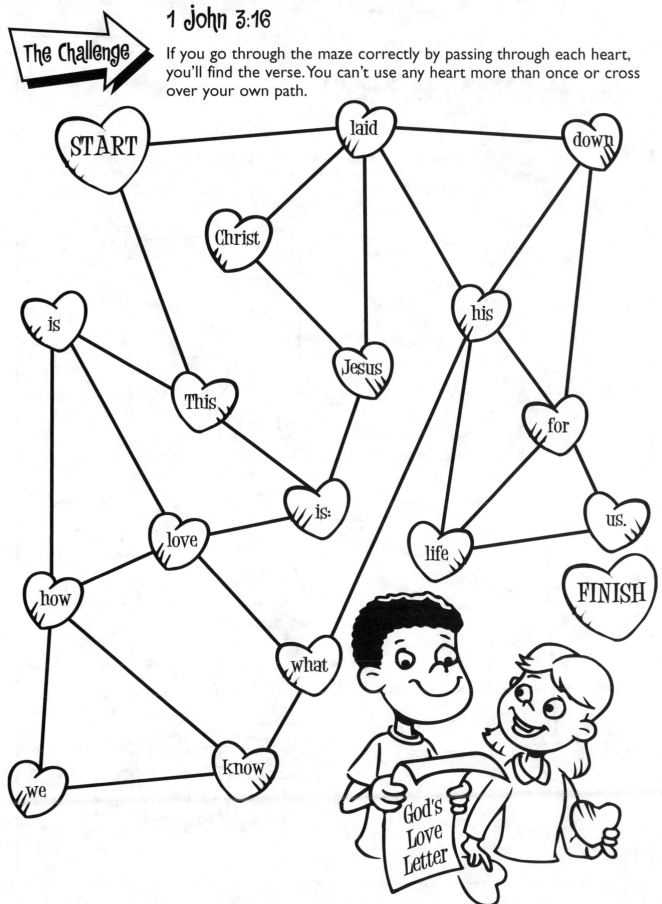

HEARTSTRINGS!

1 John 3:16

The Challenge If you go through the maze correctly by passing through each heart, you'll find the verse. You can't use any heart more than once or cross over your own path.

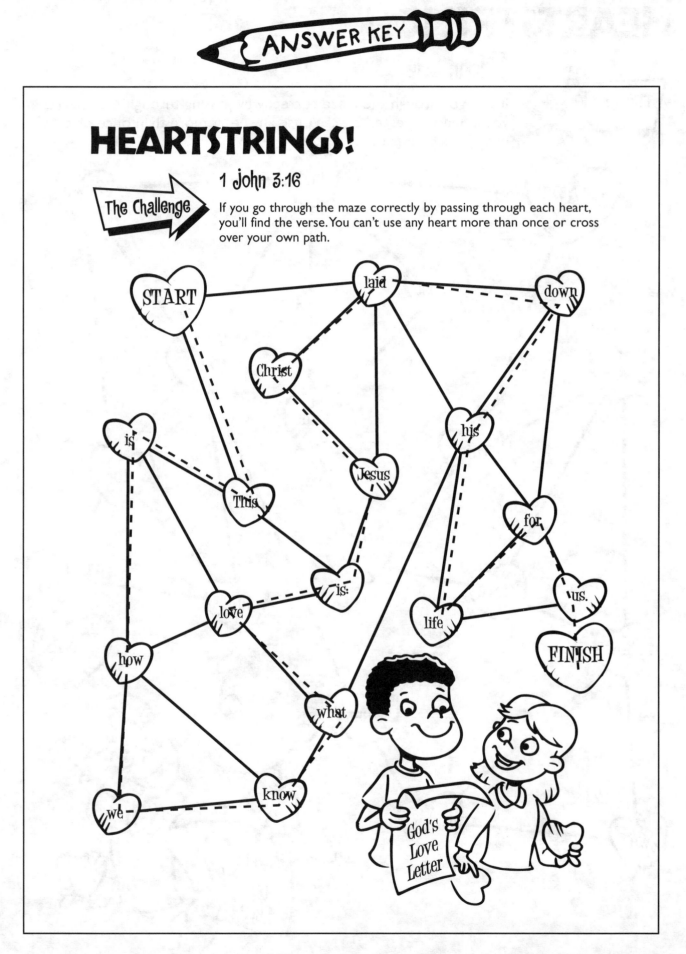

WRITE ON!

1 John 4:9

"This is how God showed his love among us: He sent his one and only Son into the world that we might live through him."

The Challenge ➤ Write the words of the verse in the crossword grid below. (Hint: Draw a line through each word as you use it and through the words already entered in the grid.)

WRITE ON!

1 John 4:9

"This is how God showed his love among us: He sent his one and only Son into the world that we might live through him."

The Challenge ▶ Write the words of the verse in the crossword grid below. (Hint: Draw a line through each word as you use it and through the words already entered in the grid.)

A-MAZE-ING LOVE

1 John 4:11

"Dear friends, since God so loved us, we also ought to love one another."

Find your way through the maze by finding the words of 1 John 4:11 in order and then try to memorize the verse!

A-MAZE-ING LOVE

The Challenge

1 John 4:11

"Dear friends, since God so loved us, we also ought to love one another."

Find your way through the maze by finding the words of 1 John 4:11 in order and then try to memorize the verse!

LIFE SUPPORT SYSTEM

1 John 5:11

The Challenge Solve this rebus telling about God's incredible gift to us.

"  -L ______  -T ______ G+5-F+N ______

 -B ______  -M+  -I ______

L +  -KN ______,  -H ______ 3rd -RD+S ______

L +  -KN ______  -FH ______

 -CH ______ 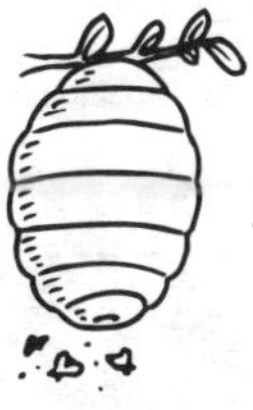 -VE+S ______  -PGE ______."

LIFE SUPPORT SYSTEM

1 john 5:11

The Challenge → Solve this rebus telling about God's incredible gift to us.

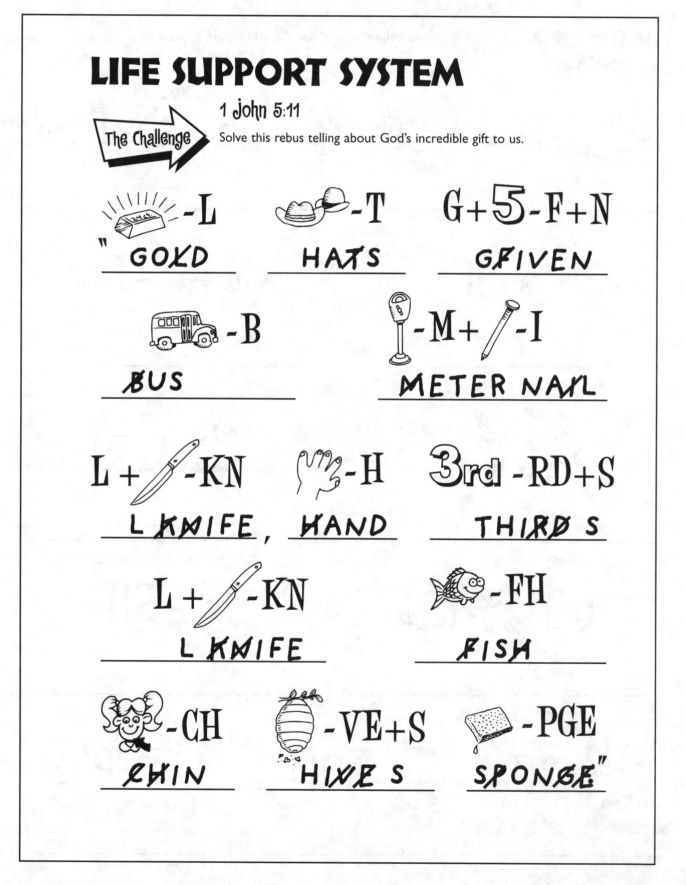

— L
" GOLD

— T
HATS

G + 5 − F + N
GIVEN

— B
BUS

− M + / − I
METER NAIL

L + / − KN
L KNIFE ,

— H
HAND

3rd − RD + S
THIRD S

L + / − KN
L KNIFE

— FH
FISH

— CH
CHIN

— VE + S
HIVE S

— PGE
SPONGE "

BUZZ WORDS!

1 John 5:20

"The Son of God has come and has given us understanding, so that we may know him who is true."

The Challenge ➡

Follow the words of the verse through the beehive. Start at the smallest bee and finish at the black one. Don't get stung by some tricky parts where words are repeated.

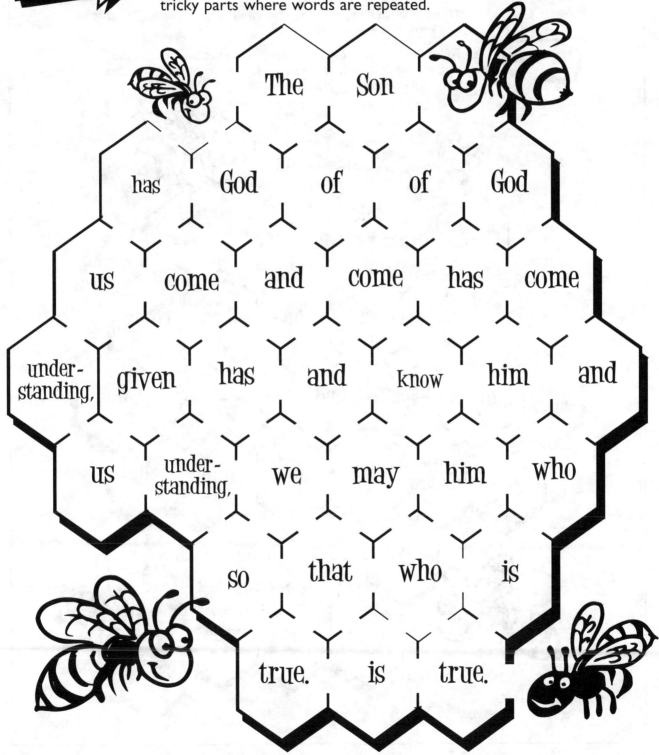

BUZZ WORDS!

1 John 5:20

"The Son of God has come and has given us understanding, so that we may know him who is true."

The Challenge → Follow the words of the verse through the beehive. Start at the smallest bee and finish at the black one. Don't get stung by some tricky parts where words are repeated.

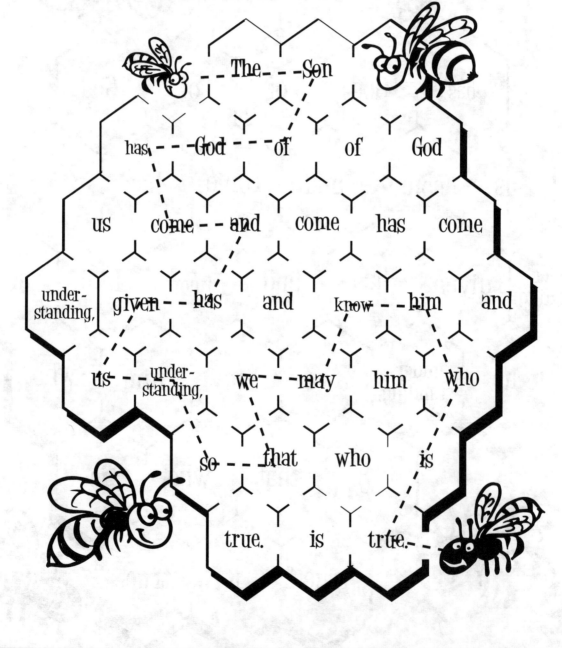